The Beading Book

The Beading Book

Julia Jones

LACIS PUBLICATIONS
Berkeley, California USA

For Esther – from Mum

Published in 1993
in the USA by
LACIS PUBLICATIONS
3136 Adeline Street
Berkeley, CA 94703

ISBN 0-916896-48-X

First published in 1993
A & C Black (Publishers) Limited
35 Bedford Row,
London WC1R 4JH

Typeset by Rowland Phototypesetting Limited,
Bury St Edmunds, Suffolk
Printed and bound in Great Britain by
Butler and Tanner Limited, Frome and London

Contents

Colour illustrations

Preface

My fascination with beads, threads and rich textiles began when, as a small child I was allowed to play with the contents of an aunt's sewing cupboard. One of my earliest memories is of sitting on the floor, surrounded by embroidery threads, beads and buttons and of my much older and very male, cousin, complaining to his mother that 'She's covered the sitting room floor again!'

It was from that homely and simple beginning that my love of crafts began. My mother and her sisters, having experienced the Depression and World War II, had learnt to 'make do and mend' and I, as the youngest member of the family, had ample opportunity to watch as women worked and gossiped.

As I watched, I picked up the rudiments of most skills. A friend of my mother's spent her lunch times teaching me to tat and to crochet. My mother despaired of teaching me to knit, but my father, taught in the Navy to knit socks, finally succeeded in instilling the basic 'knit 1, purl 1' into my fingers and my brain.

To the despair of my domestic science teachers at school (in fact the despair of most of my teachers!), I continued to delight in the spectrum of yarns, threads and fabrics available in stores and shops and like many others, I developed and still possess the magpie instinct to collect textiles. I did not, however, want to make cooking aprons and oven gloves! My goal was the exotic and the expensive!

I discovered the delight of beads as a side-effect of learning to make bobbin lace. Researching the history of English lace-making, I began to collect antique bobbins, spangled with beads from the Victorian era. Soon the emphasis of my interest shifted to the history of the beads themselves – how they were produced and their many decorative uses. Once I had seen the beautiful beaded dresses, belts and purses in many museums and textile collections all over the country, the idea for this book began to germinate. Following the instructions will enable you to create fringes, tassels, braids, heavily encrusted fabrics, or simple, elegant motifs using many different crafts and skills. Once you have begun, I am sure you will find, with surprize, that beading produces wonderful results from very basic techniques. Using simple knots, straight and back stitches, bugle and seed beads can bring a plain garment to sparkling life.

If the instructions and ideas I have produced in this book, inspire you to experiment and explore, then I shall be delighted and this will be a tribute to the patience of my mother, my aunts and countless friends over the years.

Acknowledgements

The author would like to thank the following for their help and interest in this book:

Patricia Woods of Mulberry Silks for the loan of threads for photography

Fantasy Fabrics for the loan of silks and nets for photography

Perdita and Cordelia Mellor of Perdy and Cordelia's Antique Shop, Lichfield for the loan of beaded items for photography

Maureen Murray and Charlotte Smith, The Bead Shop, London for the loan of beads for photography

Joel & Son Fabrics, London for the loan of fabrics for photography

Barbara Deer for the line drawings

Maggie Murray for the photography

and finally Esther Jones for her patience and assistance in proof reading and copywriting

1
The history of beads and beadwork

Despite their obvious popularity for adornment, it is not known precisely how and where the art of beadmaking was developed. Man has always been fascinated by shells and pebbles and the obvious use of these for personal decoration made them the ideal forerunners of the bead and sequins of the modern world.

The stringing together of beads, instead of merely wearing just one developed at a very early stage. The belief that one bead worn as a talisman offered protection against the dangers of life would be magnified many times by the wearing of a whole necklace. It is interesting to note that the Egyptian words used for amulet also mean 'protection', 'the thing that keeps safe' or 'strengthener'.

A stunning variety of beads has been produced around the world and the constructive and decorative use of beads takes many forms. Strictly speaking, only those beads that are sewn to a ground fabric can be classed as embroidery, although these may be frequently supported by wire or thread before being sewn down. The use of beads on very early textiles was limited because of the difficulties of producing a thread strong enough to resist and withstand constant friction. In addition, early beads were not considered decorative enough to embellish rich textiles, until the piercing of semi-precious stones and the manufacture of small glass beads. Professional embroiderers were quick to realize their decorative potential and they soon became essential for the best religious and royal needlework.

Previously jewels for ornamentation were simply hung round the neck or set into elaborately decorated clasps and brooches, designed to hold together capes or mantles. Early beadwork was strictly limited to ecclesiastical embroideries, the robes of royalty and the regalia of state. Magnificent jewel-studded armour became a powerful status symbol, the privilege of wealth and royal or noble birth. So significant did the wearing of jewellery become that laws were passed regulating its use.

Early medieval bead embroidery was worked with gold and silver thread for ecclesiastical vestments and church furnishings, often combined with other decorative and precious materials, such as pearls and coral. The famous Opus

Anglicanum (English metallic thread embroidery) of this period was distinguished by the beaded outlines of its saintly figures. Sadly these beaded outlines have been lost and rows of running stitches mark their loss. A fragment of this fabric remains in the tenth century collection of Saint Cuthbert's vestments, now housed in Durham Cathedral, England.

Seed pearls and beads were used in the Germany of the twelfth century to produce church vestments of parchment. While in the thirteenth and fourteenth centuries, larger beads decorated the vellum covers of the elaborately designed religious books so indicative of the country and the period.

Tudor and Stuart England saw the emergence of the fashion for wearing beads on clothing. Precious gems were often sewn to garments to prevent theft and to provide personal adornment. The production of fine steel, replacing the clumsy iron needles of previous centuries, facilitated more delicate designwork, and enabled tiny beads and seed pearls to be sewn to the court dress of both men and women.

During the second quarter of the seventeenth century small, square bags were fashionable, usually embroidered with repeating patterns or flower motifs. These were given as tokens of esteem and as such were highly prized.

Also popular at this time was a distinctive form of raised beadwork, often featuring the use of seed pearls. Consisting of richly decorative bas-relief stitching, stumpwork was combined with appliqué work, forming panels, mirror frames, cabinets and baskets. Metallic thread was cleverly stitched over wadding or wood block padding to produce a three-dimensional effect. Surviving caskets vary considerably in size and quality, but all have highly distinctive lids and intricate interiors. Designs usually incorporate a central canopy depicting figures, castles and trees, birds and beasts, all surrounded by deep floral borders.

The cream satin ground most widely used for this work was always backed with linen, the working outline either being drawn directly in black ink or traced with some form of carbon. The embroidery of this time was of a highly decorative quality, employing as it did such materials as lustrous and brightly coloured silks, pearls, beads and jewels, paper, cord, gimp threads and silver plate. The transparent form of the mineral 'mica' was used to represent windows, silver plate imitated water and irridescent feathers were cunningly shaped to form birds. Vast numbers of multi-coloured beads were threaded onto wire, producing whole panels, frames for mirrors and even ingeniously complex baskets. Beads were laboriously sewn onto panels one by one, often with very little attention being given to design or direction. This was considered a suitable occupation for well-bred young girls, the more artistic of whom produced high quality mosaic work and even tiny beadwork gardens within the lids of their boxes.

Beads were in great demand and even the crewel work hangings of the eighteenth century had their designs enlivened by the use of beads, emphasizing the strongest design features. The magnificent wall hangings at Knebworth House in Hertfordshire are worked with backgrounds of fine beads, outlining the overall design of trees.

Beadwork has continued to be exceedingly popular in France for centuries. Bookbindings in particular often show exquisite workmanship. A distinctive 'sablé' purse could contain as many as 1,000 tiny beads to the square inch (2.5 cm²). These were strung in the correct pattern order and laid across a framework, to be linked by tiny stitches. (The word sablé means 'sandy' or 'covered with sand'.)

Meanwhile, across the whole of Europe court dress was becoming increasingly elaborate. Gems and spangles (sequins) were combined with fine silks and gold threads to produce ever more flamboyant embroidery.

However, dress fashion inevitably became simpler, and beadwork was eventually confined to accessories. Beaded flat pumps were popular for ladies during the eighteenth century. Beaded bags and purses took the place of pockets, and these were further decorated with tassels and looped fringes. The reappearance of pockets in the nineteenth century did nothing to diminish the popularity of beaded bags and these can still be admired today.

The development of chemical dyeing led to the craze for Berlin woolwork that was to sweep Europe and America during the 1830s. Bright and often garish yarns were produced in a wide range of colours and patterns, pictures and prints were distributed in vast numbers. Berlin woolwork owed its success to its ease of production. Needlewomen in Europe and America could safely embark upon a design, confident in the knowledge that a small amount of skill was required to produce adequate results. Tent stitch was exclusively used and this simple stitch, often combined with small beads in toning colours, created a huge variety of household objects (see colour illustration on page 38). An enormous demand for regularly shaped and coloured beads resulted – the finest quality beads at that time being imported from France. Suppliers of tapestry wools for this unprecedented boom were quick to notice the additional demand and soon stocked tiny bottles of beads to tempt the embroiderer.

Fine and medium-sized beads were used for all types of canvas work. These were sold by weight and were known as 'pound' beads. In America coloured glass beads were popular for further embellishing the finished work adding, where possible, decorative cords, tassels and fringes. In Great Britain, Victorian ingenuity found uses for beads on items as diverse and unlikely as scripture mottos and candlesticks. These were not always well designed and as the nineteenth century drew to a close standards in all forms of embroidery deteriorated considerably, despite the efforts of designers such as William Morris and the members of the Arts and Crafts movement.

The industrial revolution had brought great changes to all aspects of manufacturing, including beadmaking. In the 1890s an attempt was made to produce a machine for applying beads. However, the irregularity of bead sizes and shapes proved a severe problem. Eventually success was achieved with the introduction of Cornely's revolutionary new machine. This single-thread machine was able to work a chain stitch, the direction of which was controlled manually. The machine could be adapted to chain, couch, cord, braid or even apply threaded beads and sequins, using a self-looping thread and universal feed. Such was the brilliance of this invention, that the machine is still in regular use in the fashion industry making sumptuous embroidered and heavily beaded fabrics.

Meanwhile, the inspired use of the tambour hook in France to apply beads led to the development of a flourishing trade in trimmings both for high fashion and for household goods. These trimmings were produced by outworkers in their own homes for depressingly inadequate wages.

The emancipation of women and the introduction of the outrageous 'flapper' dresses of the 1920s led to the European heyday of beads and beading. Heavy beads were attached to light, flimsy fabrics such as silk and georgette. Unfortunately, the fabric of many of these garments has disintegrated, a process hastened no doubt by the weight of beads. The most famous and desirable dresses of the time were those made by the Italian designer Fortuny, whose distinctive tiny pleats were each weighted with hand-painted Venetian glass beads.

Despite World War II the fashion for beaded evening wear continued and this was produced for the wealthy patrons of the French fashion houses. Then the popularity of beading seriously declined. The 1980s saw a revival of interest in the use of the tambour hook for beading and this was echoed in the renewed use of this technique in the fashion trade. Modern production techniques and the work of specialist designers seems to have renewed popularity of beading in all its forms and needleworkers are again incorporating beautiful and colourful beads in all forms of textile work.

2
Types of beads and how they are made

Early man first discovered stone for weapons and as a substance ideally suited for use in personal adornment and decoration. However, in those far off days its applications were fairly limited. Naturally stones which already had holes were greatly prized, as they could be both attached to garments or worn as pendants.

It was not until the invention of the awl that man was able to produce stones drilled to his own requirements. However, as the awl was powered only by the palms of the hands, its use was limited to easily drilled substances such as soft stones, wood and seeds. The subsequent development of the more powerful bow-drill meant that holes could be drilled in much harder substances, even in materials such as granite and marble.

The earliest surviving drilled beads were discovered recently in Upper Egypt, during the excavation of the Baderian graves. Here small pieces of stone had been chipped to the required size and shape. A hole was drilled through the middle of each and they were rounded by rolling between pieces of harder, flattened and more abrasive stone. The beads could then be strung together to form cylindrical necklaces and bracelets.

Beads have been made from many different substances with great success. Much of their attraction stems from the variety of styles, colours and shapes. Natural and man-made materials are still being employed today, often using the methods of the past and a selection of readily available beads are described here.

Beads made from natural materials

Amber

Amber is an organic gemstone, surrounded by legend and mystery, and derived from trees fossilized millions of years ago. Mined today in Burma, Sicily, Romania, Poland and Mexico, amber has been carved and shaped since pre-historic times. It varies in colour from yellow to reddish brown and can contain insects and foliage trapped as the resin hardened. Soft and warm to the touch amber will float in salty water. When touched with a hot needle, amber smells fragrant. The Greeks believed it was formed from solidified tears or from the essence of the sun's rays 'congealed in the sea and cast upon the shore'.

Bamboo

These beads are cylindrical and are made from the hollow stalk of the bamboo. They are useful in modern, experimental embroidery work.

Bone

Bone can be left in its natural state or dyed black or white. It is a more acceptable substitute for ivory in jewellery and textiles.

Coconut

Coconut beads are usually round or irregularly shaped washers. They are naturally cream in colour, but can be dyed. They can also be waxed to give a smoother finish, which feels slightly oily when handled.

Copal

Copal is a semi-fossilized resin which is cheaper than amber.

Coral

Coral is the skeleton of sea creatures, composed of calcium carbonate. It is found in warm, shallow waters. Precious coral is a hard substance, easy to carve and polish. The coral of the Mediterranean Sea is still worked using methods employed during the Middle Ages.

Horn

Beads can be made from the horns of many animals. To test whether horn or bone beads are genuine, lightly touch the inside of the hole with a heated needle. Horn and bone will smell quite unlike hot plastic.

Ivory

Ivory is the hard cream-coloured tusk of the elephant. Until 1870 Dieppe, in France, was the centre of the European ivory carving trade and many beads were produced there. However, modern ethical thinking on conservation has led to a ban on the use of this substance. So if ivory is to be used at all, only antique beads should be employed.

Jet

Jet comes from the fossilized wood of an ancient variety of Monkey Puzzle Tree, which grew some 180 million years ago. Hard jet was formed beneath the sea under enormous pressure, while soft jet was produced under the much lower pressure of fresh water rivers and lakes. Hard jet is very durable and easily worked, but soft jet is much more likely to crack as it is shaped.

Jet can be found in many parts of the world, but the most famous source is Whitby in Yorkshire, home of the finest examples. During the Middle Ages, craftsmen made rosaries for the monks of Whitby Abbey, but it was not until the invention of the precision lathe in the nineteenth century that the flourishing jet industry arose. The industry was also influenced by the death of Victoria's consort, Prince Albert, an event which led to a fashion for mourning jewellery, giving the home industry a great boost. So great did this demand become that soft jet was imported from France and Spain to produce even more beads. Imitation jet was made from bog oak and even from black glass. This is still described as 'French jet'. Man-made imitations were later produced from vulcanite and bakelite.

Lac

The multicoloured 'Lac' beads of Northern India are made from a resinous substance produced by the trees which house the 'lac' insect.

Marble

This mineral is not usually associated with beads today, but in the past it has been highly polished to display its distinctive grain and in such a form it does make very attractive beads.

Meerschaum

'Meerschaum' is German for 'sea foam' and describes a light porous stone which is found floating on the surface of the sea. Also known as 'gypsum', it can be carved and polished with wax.

Sea urchin

Looking like shell or ceramic pendants, the spines of the sea urchin can be used to make beautiful and dramatic earrings.

Seeds

Prehistoric man used small seeds as jewellery. However, seeds and plant material offer scope for experimenting with many ancient techniques which can still be relevant to needleworkers today. A look at traditional ethnic embroidery from many cultures will offer sources of tremendous inspiration.

The Karen women of Thailand used shiny white seeds known as 'Job's tears' to decorate jackets which were worn only by married women. Originally designed as a status symbol, these seeds are worked with embroidery stitches to produce many varied and charming patterns.

In Java the 'rudraksha' nut is used for making Hindu prayer beads. While many seeds, such as those of the watermelon, can be used to produce necklaces and earrings.

Shells

Shells as decorative objects were the forerunners of much of today's jewellery. They could be drilled and shaped to produce dramatic effects. In many cultures monetary worth was often assigned to certain shells, as in the Solomon Islands, where the sacred red shells (attributed to the gods), became more valuable than the more common white varieties.

The use of shells for adornment stretches back through time. As early as the first century AD the tribes of the Mississippi basin made large shell breastplates engraved with mythical beasts as symbols of their warlike prowess.

For use as jewellery, large shells were usually broken into pieces and roughly chipped to a circular shape. A hole was drilled in the middle of each disc using an awl or bow drill and a series of these were then threaded on to a thin stick. This cylinder of discs was rolled backwards and forwards by hand on an abrasive stone until each was smooth, round and of uniform size. The North American Indians perfected this method for shaping white and purple clam shells into 'wampum' – shell discs of great value. Besides forming a unit of currency, they were also used to convey messages between distant tribes. At important ceremonies, belts worn by tribal chiefs were decorated with wampum.

Abalone

Various shells are still popular for modern beadwork. These include the reddish abalone shells from the South Seas and the beautiful blue abalone known as 'paua' from New Zealand.

Cowrie

Of all the shells used as currencies, cowrie is perhaps the most widely known. Oval in shape and creamy white in colour, the cowrie shell is mottled with brown spots and bands. They can often be found many thousands of miles from their natural waters. In parts of Africa for instance they were included in the price paid for a bride, while elsewhere they became part of the regalia donned by warriors as certain protection in battle. Many cultures still consider the cowrie a symbol of fertility and they are combined with glass beads sewn to ground fabrics to be worn by both marriagable young men and women.

Mother-of-pearl

Mother-of-pearl is the iridescent lining of a shell, usually that of the Australian pearl oyster, which can be carved into beads and pendants. Tiny pieces can also be glued with great care to large wooden base beads or used as an inlay, producing mosaic effects.

Mother-of-pearl can be used in its natural form or dyed many different, deeper colours. The most common bead shapes are round, tulip or rice. Pendants include many varied and unusual shapes – star, love bird, heart, seagull, leaf, cross, eagle, mushroom, fish, shell, elephant, crescent moon, dolphin, seahorse and teddy bear. These are usually pierced or designed to hang from a loop.

Pearls

Natural pearls are formed from the protective secretions of the oyster or the freshwater mussel produced to surround foreign bodies such as grit which have accidentally lodged in the shell. Cultured pearls are formed by the deliberate introduction of such an irritant.

Seed pearls are produced by the freshwater mussel and are gathered from streams, rivers and lakes. During the Middle Ages these were collected in vast quantities, to be combined with richly textured embroidery. Portraits of the Tudor monarchs of England bear testimony to the love they had for personal adornment of this type.

Fresh-water pearls, considerably less expensive than cultured pearls, are nubbly and creamy white in colour.

Natural pearls vary in colour from creamy white through to brown and can be bleached or dyed to improve their appearance. Formed from layers of nacre, no two pearls are the same in shape or colour. Pearls are weighed in grains – one grain equalling 0.05 g. A seed pearl weighs less than 0.016 g.

The Russian Imperial Royal family were addicted to the use of pearls. Their robes were often so heavily encrusted that sitting comfortably must have proved difficult. Even Russian peasant girls coveted pearls and they wore them looped and embroidered on their wedding dresses.

In India, princes adopted European fashion, wearing crowns embroidered with glass beads, sequins and seed pearls. Piercing a hole in such small pearls was a delicate operation. Wax was used to hold each pearl in place, while the hole was drilled very carefully using a fine bow drill. These pearl beads were generally combined with gemstones and embroidery or strung into elaborate nets to be applied to rich fabrics.

The love of pearls has continued into this century. One American society hostess, Mrs Frederick Vanderbilt, received her guests in a gown embellished with £50,000 worth of pearls. While another of her contemporaries, received scathing criticism in the press for her extravagent pearl necklaces and pearl-embroidered dresses, which were said to have been valued at one million dollars each in 1910!

Tiger shell

Dramatic effects can be achieved by using the dark mottled 'tiger' shell for modern embroidery and jewellery.

Wood

Bog oak

This fossilized wood is found in the Irish peat bogs. It has a dark brown, dull finish. Bog oak was enamelled in the 1880s and used as a cheap imitation jet.

Cinnabar

Cinnabar is a vermilion-coloured wood from China and Japan, which can be hand-carved with crisp geometric patterns. Many attractive and unusual shapes are available, but these lend themselves more readily to jewellery than embroidery.

Cork

Cork beads are formed from the thick, porous outer bark of the cork oak tree.

Ebony

Ebony is a hard black wood which can be carved or inlaid with metal. Beads come in many shapes such as washers, cubes and rounds.

Hardwood

English hardwood beads of sycamore, elm, cherry and oak are always popular. They can be varnished, stained or carved and even painted in the form of birds and animals.

Palm wood

Palm wood, cream in colour with brown lines, is used to produce washers, round or oval beads.

Red wood

Red wood is a close-grained wood from Canada. Beads can range in colour from cream and pale yellow to a warm rusty red.

Soft wood

These beads are usually round and range in size from 25 mm to 50 mm (1–2 in). They are particularly useful in teaching co-ordination and threading skills to children. They can, of course, be painted or left in their natural state.

Soft wood, painted

Soft wooden painted beads come in many shapes, including washers, flat discs, round, semi-spherical, oval, square and tubular.

Man-made beads

Glass

There are two types of glass bead made by hand – those made from a hollow tube of blown glass or wound beads made from a heated glass rod. Wound beads were made by the Egyptians from about 1400 BC. In Bohemia and India 'lamp' beads are made by melting and shaping the glass rod over a lamp flame. Fine decoration is then painted onto the bead with a molten glass filament.

Crystal

These are not natural crystals but lead glass cut to shape. See page 51 for further details.

Drawn-cane

Drawn-cane beads are made from layers of coloured glass in rods which are heated, thinly drawn out to a great length and then cut into beads. Included in this category are patterns such as the star, rosetta and chevron.

Millefiori

Complex 'millefiori' (a thousand flowers) or mosaic work was probably developed around 1000 BC. Tiny slices of fine multi-coloured glass cane are fused to a glass bead.

Mould-cast

A glass cane is heated until soft and then segments are put into a bead-shaped mould, which is closed until the glass cools.

Wound

The bead is formed by letting molten glass wind round a heated metal rod or wire which is continuously rotated. At intervals the bead is rolled on a flat metal surface to give it the required shape. The gold stripes and swirls on some beads are made with 'goldstone' – also known as 'aventurine'. This is a type of Venetian glass which contains tiny spangles of mica or haematite.

Lamp beads sometimes contain silver foil which has been applied to the central glass core. Ultra transparent glass is then trailed over it. Any exposed silver will oxidize in time, giving the beads a fine antique look. By entirely coating the foil with glass, a deep lustrous effect can be achieved.

Metal

Beads can be made in gold, silver or platinum and also from copper and brass. Copper and brass beads can be plated with silver or gold or decorated with 'cloisonné'. Cloisonné is a technique where wire-enclosed shapes are painted with coloured enamels before being fired.

Objets trouvés (found objects)

In Victorian times, and again in the 1960s, it became fashionable to incorporate many different small and unusual objects into embroidery. Drift wood and bones were included in the more experimental pieces. Inventive Victorians even worked with sequins made from fishscales, which were laboriously cleaned and pierced before use.

It is possible to include many manufactured items in a piece of embroidery. The more obvious buttons and fastenings could be incorporated along with mechanical parts, bottle tops and other industrial bric-a-brac. Dried pulses of all descriptions can also be included, as well as the vast array of pasta manufactured in many different shapes and colours.

Paper

Paper beads can be made at home using cheap materials and can produce an attractive bead. See page 127 for instructions.

Plastic

Plastic beads come in a wide range of transparent or opaque colours, including gold and silver, black and white.

Plastic is a modern material derived from oil. It was first invented in Britain in the mid-nineteenth century to imitate natural materials such as horn, tortoiseshell, coral, wood and ivory as supplies of these became more scarce and, therefore, more expensive. A form of plastic was first patented in 1861 by Henry Parkes.

Plastic beads come in many forms, colours and finishes, including metallic. They are light and inexpensive and do not break easily. Chosen carefully they can be included to good effect in many modern needlework projects.

Bakelite

Bakelite – a hard thermoset plastic, which was invented in 1909 and was a forerunner of modern plastics.

Perspex

Perspex is the name given by ICI to plexiglass. It is tough transparent plastic, which is much lighter than glass. Perspex does not splinter.

Pottery

Early beads made of clay were left unfired and so disintegrated very rapidly. However, the invention of the firing process meant that they became much more durable and could be decorated with incised patterns and colour. Small pieces of clay were moulded in the hand and then pierced with a stick, which would burn away during firing. In a later development clay was pressed into a variety of shaped moulds. As well as incised decoration, patterns were worked by scratching through a contrasting outer layer of coloured clay slip, to reveal the body colour beneath.

The invention of the kiln meant that higher firing temperatures were possible and porcelain beads were produced from fine china clay. Glazes were also introduced, giving a gloss and colour never seen before.

Chinese porcelain

The Chinese first used cobalt oxide to produce blue-coloured ceramics during the Tang dynasty (eighth century AD), thus establishing what was to become a long tradition of distinctive blue and white porcelain.

Egyptian paste

This is a mixture of clay and glaze materials used by the Egyptians to make beads, charms and vessels. A particularly successful colour was copper turquoise which was used as a cheap substitute for real turquoise. The mixture could be rolled out like dough and cut into shapes or pressed into moulds.

Rose petal

These beads were popular in the seventeenth and eighteenth centuries. They are relatively easy to make at home and provide a delightful scent. For instructions on how to make the beads see page 126.

Salt dough

These beads are cheap and simple to make. A wide variety of beads can be made, which can be painted and varnished to give a very individual bead. See page 125 for instructions on how to make salt dough beads.

Vulcanite

Beads made from vulcanite were popular around 1900 and were a cheap substitute for jet. Composed of a hardened vulcanized rubber, they could be coloured by the addition of various chemicals.

3
Sequins and metallic thread

For many centuries, tiny metal discs have been pierced and sewn onto fabric. Their undoubted decorative qualities have always made them ideal objects for use in embroidery for both secular and religious purposes.

To appreciate the popularity of this form of decoration, it is necessary to visit one of the many textile collections (see list in appendix). Elizabethan and Jacobean court costume gives some idea of the ubiquitous use of sequins of all descriptions during these times. Besides being a fashion feature, they were incorporated into the elaborate and distinctive embroidered stumpwork boxes and panels, which were particularly in vogue during the Stuart era.

Indeed, during the seventeenth and eighteenth centuries, many different shapes of sequin were manufactured and these were in great demand, particularly when combined with metal thread embroidery for court gowns. The most decorative of these may have been 'papillons' (butterflies), which were stamped from sheets of silver, colour co-ordinated to match the threads used for surface embroidery.

Nowadays sequins are usually manufactured from cellulose or plastic, which has often been coated with a metallic finish. However, very early examples were almost always made from precious metal. These were referred to as 'laminae' and were cut and shaped from thin sheets of gold or silver. Their glitter added texture and richness to textiles, when applied to opulent ground fabric or used as heavy edgings or fringes. Some of the earliest references associate their use with the Phrygians, but there is also evidence pointing to their use in the many societies where craftsmen worked precious metals.

Hand-cutting of less precious metals is still practised for use on ethnic and regional embroidery, particularly in the Middle East and India. Although metals have been largely replaced by synthetic materials, shapes and colours remain remarkably traditional.

More recent interest in sequins and beads for textile decoration came with the fashion revolution of the late nineteenth and early twentieth centuries, when Paris became the artistic and fashion capital of the world. 1909 saw the appearance of the sensational Ballet Russe. The effect of Serge Diaghilev's stunning productions was to influence the fashion industry for many years. Particularly splendid were the exotic costumes designed by Léon Bakst, with their bold colours and designs, utilising sumptuous fabrics, which were further embellished with beads and sequins.

The appeal to fashion designers was immediate, evening dresses were overlaid with metallic lace and sequins or beads were applied following the main design motifs. Fragile beaded and sequinned fabrics often supported more than nine pounds of beads. This weight was to help keep the straight, tubular lines of the 'flapper' dresses so characteristic of the 1920s.

After World War I couture fashion houses, in order to distance themselves from the mass market, became distinguishable by their use of embroidery, trimmings and design. The discovery of the treasures of Tutankhamen's tomb opened up the splendours of Egyptian design to the masses. The dramatic use of colour was a notable characteristic of this excitement. (See colour illustration on page 111 of beaded net from the 1920s.) The jazz craze sweeping Europe and America encouraged the use of beads and sequins on dresses designed to be seen to best effect on the dance floor.

However, the boom could not last and the austerity of World War II sadly led to a decline in the use of heavily decorated fabrics. Beaded textiles were 'out'.

Fortunately in recent years renewed interest and new manufacturing techniques have again led to the use of sequinned fabrics for evening wear – a revival which looks likely to equal or even surpass that of the 1920s.

Sequins can be found in many shapes and colours, both traditional and modern.

Sequin

The 'chekeen' or 'sequin' was originally a Venetian gold coin of high value, used for trade with the Far East, at the end of the eighteenth century. Today, however, we use the generic term sequin to describe any metal decoration of this type. Cup sequins are more correctly described as 'couvettes', although that term is little used.

A selection of sequins

Paillette

Paillette is the technical term for a sequin but is also a small piece of coloured foil used in enamel painting. The term 'paillette' was originally applied by the French to any circular disc with a hole in its centre. Its use in the English language was first recorded in the nineteenth century.

Early metal spangle with cut radius

Spangles

These are made by coiling metal wire round a wooden or metal core. The wound coil is then cut along its length to produce a number of wire rings. These are hammered flat to form discs with a central hole and a side slit. Spangles like these have been made since medieval times.

   During the reign of the Tudor monarchs any such small circular disc or eyelet was known as a 'spangle' or an 'owe' ('oe'). These were particularly popular for use on the elaborate court dresses of both men and women of the time.

Beetles wings

The wing cases of tiny dark and iridescent beetles were pierced with a small hole at either end and stitched to textiles, usually combined with embroidery. This technique originated on the Indian sub-continent and was exported to America and Britain during the nineteenth century. Spangles can now be purchased which imitate these wing cases, but for ease of manufacture their holes are now placed, not at the tips of the wings but on either of the longer sides.

Fish scale embroidery

To the modern needleworker, the popularity of using the scales of coarse fish for embroidered work may seem a trifle bizarre! During the nineteenth century there was a great interest in all things exotic, resulting no doubt from the interest in the travels of the explorers of the times. The incomprehensible desire to employ various animal remains in unusual and decorative ways seems slightly strange to modern tastes, but a Victorian gentlewoman might amuse herself during a quiet afternoon by arranging fish scales and shaped shells on rich satins and silks to depict flowers or birds. The washed, dried and pierced scales were usually arranged in curves and circles, and were selected according to size or type. These were incorporated into embroidery designs to form flower heads or to suggest feathers. They were often used to represent the fronds of maidenhair fern. Classic and geometric designs proved to be universally popular and the technique was used on many household items. Obviously the frailty of the scales meant that this skill could only be applied to items subjected to very little wear, and which would not require washing.

   Modern sequins and sew-on celluloid or pressed acetate shapes are often reminiscent of fish scales in texture and colour and are doubtless a more acceptable substitute. They can be carefully chosen and applied to reproduce the design concepts of the nineteenth century.

Mother-of-pearl work

To produce this work, small pieces of mother-of-pearl, probably button maker's waste, were trimmed into small shapes and perforated to sew onto rich backgrounds. Fine detail was added to the design by embroidering with metallic thread or silks. Although button maker's waste is not readily available today, mother-of-pearl buttons are still used to form the designs on the coats of London's pearly kings and queens.

'Ecaille' or 'stamped quillwork'

This was a cheaper imitation of mother-of-pearl work, utilizing flattened bird's quills.

Melon seed embroidery

Seeds of many kinds are used as decoration in tribal costumes and are featured in 'free' embroidery. As vegetable material cannot be pierced once it has dried, seeds must be pierced and strung on waxed linen thread. They should be washed if at all sticky and thoroughly dried before use.

Pale seeds can be dyed by part drying them, before immersing in a hot dye bath. Polishing or waxing will help preserve seeds, making them more pleasant to handle.

If they are to be incorporated in a modern embroidery design, be aware of shape. For instance, geometric patterns can be achieved by threading melon seeds onto attractive yarns, using them for couching or even knitting. Dried, unpierced seeds can be applied to a ground fabric by placing them under transparent fabric, and then sewn in position with hand or machine embroidery.

Trimmings

Ready made sequin trimmings are now available, incorporating different embroidery techniques and these can be used to good effect when time is short. Alternately second-hand dealers and antique fairs can be a source of Victorian and Edwardian trimmings which can be restored to their former glory and incorporated into embroidery and fashion garments. Care must be taken, however, when laundering these items and reference should be made to Chapter 11 on the care and conservation of beaded fabrics.

A recent innovation is the manufacture of iron-on diamanté and pearl trimmings. These can be purchased from the craft departments in many shops. Manufacturer's instructions should be followed with great care, particularly in respect of application and of washing methods to ensure that no damage is caused either to the trimmings or to the fabric of the garment. Individual crystals and pearl trimmings come in a variety of widths and sizes. They are usually attached to strips of paper and sold by the metre or yard. Individual motifs are cut out, positioned on the fabric and pressed in position with a warm iron.

Metallic threads

Metallic threads are often used in conjunction with sequins and spangles to increase their decorative effect.

The use of metallic threads has been known for centuries. In very early times pure gold was beaten into thin sheets, known as 'aurum battatum'. This was then carefully cut into fine strips. These gold strips were sufficiently thin and pliable to enable weavers to work them into the warp of fine fabrics. They could also be stitched through open weaves or wound round a silken core to be couched (positioned and fastened using another thread) in place.

Later much finer gold strips were wound round silken cores to produce thread of the type found in the famous embroideries of the Opus Anglicanum. The gold sheet for the thread on vestments of this period is an amazing 0.25 mm (0.001 in) thick and this was cut into strips which are between 2 mm (0.083 in) and 3 mm (0.1 in) wide. The resulting hand-made thread is just over 1 mm (0.05 in) thick.

An alternative technique for incorporating gold work into embroidery was burnishing. Gold leaf was reduced in thickness by being beaten between pieces of thin vellum. Several layers would be placed together for a final beating – the work continuing until the required thickness was achieved. The fine gold sheet was then applied to animal membranes, which could finally be cut into thin strips.

Modern gold-plated wire is formed by first moulding, heating and cooling, and then forging a silver bar. The bar is drawn and polished before being wrapped with gold foil. After burnishing, the bar is drawn through progressively smaller holes until the required gauge of wire is produced. Very fine wire is formed and polished at high speed. To produce 'Jap' or other wound threads the wire has to be flattened through rollers before being spun onto a silk or synthetic core yarn.

'Jap' gold thread is the modern substitute for 'aurum battatum'. Its colour can vary from a pale, almost greenish hue to rich vibrant oranges and reds. The tone is controlled by the colour of the silk or rayon core employed. 'Jap' thread cannot be worked with a needle, as this would result in the gold being stripped from the core yarn. It must, therefore, be couched into position. A study of early couching techniques will show how much variety of texture can be obtained by varying the angle of the threads, enabling the needleworker to produce gleaming ridges and spirals or continuous smooth and glossy surfaces.

The wide variety of thicknesses and textures of modern gold and silver threads can be used to great effect with sequins of all descriptions, working either in toning or contrasting colours. Do be sure to use a metallic thread specifically produced for embroidery when attaching sequins, as wound threads will be stripped of their metal. For particularly rich textural effects, however, couched gold or silver threads can be combined with sequins and beads in an endless variety of ways.

Methods for applying sequins

Sequins can be purchased in many different colours, either pre-packaged in bubble packs or plastic tubs, or strung together like a necklace. Always make sure to buy sufficient sequins to complete your chosen design, as colours do vary from dye lot to dye lot.

Sequins can be applied singly, or in rows, motifs or groups on most fabrics. There are several methods of application, either by needle or by the use of the tambour hook. If an original design is required, find a suitable shape either from a magazine, photograph or postcard and trace this onto good quality tracing paper, using a sharp HB lead pencil. The design can then be transferred to the fabric, either using dressmaker's carbon paper, or the prick and pounce method (see pages 45–46).

Attaching single sequins

Sequins with a central hole are best sewn down with a matching or contrasting thread. Silver or gold can, however, look most effective. Sequins to be sewn in rows can be attached using a single back stitch.

Method 1

1 Fasten on thread.

2 Bring needle through fabric from back of work and through central hole of first sequin.

3 Take a short horizontal straight stitch to the right across the radius of the sequin.

4 Take the needle to the back of work.

5 Take a straight stitch 1½ sequins wide horizontally to the left, through the fabric and through the central hole of the second sequin.

6 Sew down the second sequin with a straight stitch to the right, as before.

7 Repeat as necessary.

Method 1 – applying single sequins in rows

Method 2

1 Secure the first sequin with a straight stitch to the right, as in method 1 (see 1–4).

2 Take the needle behind the sequin and through the fabric to the left edge of this first sequin.

3 Take the needle down again through its central hole.

4 Take the needle behind the work a sequin's width to the left and attach the second sequin in the same manner. There will be two stitches in each hole and the sequins will just touch.

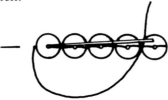

Method 2 – applying single sequins in rows

Overlapping sequins

1 Fasten on thread and attach first sequin as described in method one, taking needle to back of work.

2 Place second sequin in position, so it just overlaps the first sequin.

3 Take needle behind sequins, bringing it through fabric and central hole of second sequin.

4 Straight stitch to the right edge of second sequin and take needle to back of work.

5 Repeat as required.

Overlapping sequins

Sequins in the shape of shells, leaves and flowers

Sewing down sequin shapes

Shaped sequins

Unusual or irregularly shaped sequins should be sewn down with tiny straight stitches. Embroidery jewels in metallic mounts should be attached using the same method.

Sewing sequins with a small bead

1 Bring the thread through the fabric, central hole of the sequin and the small bead.

2 Take the thread back down through the sequin and fabric.

3 Repeat as required.

Sequins and beads can be sewn in many combinations, separately or in rows.

Sewing a sequin with a small bead

Sewing sequin waste

In modern embroidery 'sequin waste' has been put to good use. This term is applied to the remaining flat, perforated sheets from which sequins have been cut. It can now be purchased from craft shops and department stores and can be obtained in a variety of colours and finishes. Small, shaped areas can be cut from these sheets and applied to fabric in conjunction with beads or metallic thread embroidery to produce dramatic effects.

1 Cut into the required shapes, avoiding sharp angles where possible.

2 Sew down with a toning thread at intervals using tiny straight stitches. Use just enough stitches to keep the shape firmly in position.

Metallic thread can be used to good effect, adding another decorative dimension to the work.

Attaching sequin waste

Tambouring

Tambouring provides a quick and effective method of applying beads and sequins to fabric.

(Methods of applying both beads and sequins with a tambouring hook are explained in detail in Chapter 7.)

Kathiawar embroidery

The Kathiawar district of western India produces a lavish and glamorous form of embroidery, which is used to decorate delicate garments and veils, as well as domestic textiles and cattle trappings. It is characterized by the use of small circles of glass, known as 'shisha', which are combined with long, close, darning stitches. The main influence on this work seems to be the colourful embroidery of the Punjab. The stitches rely for effect on the contrast between the dense, matt, highly textured areas and the light, translucent ground fabrics used for the skirts and veils of the women and children. 'Shisha' mirrors add weight, helping the fabric to drape and flow. Shisha mirrors can be blanket stitched in place through small holes round their circumference, or held by long straight stitches. It is customary for a young Kathiawar girl to wrap her trousseau in a square of embroidery known as a 'chakla'. After the marriage this 'chakla' will hang on the wall of her new home.

In common with many traditional crafts, all pieces of Kathiawar embroidery have a tiny corner deliberately left unfinished, as it was believed that only God could attain perfection. Therefore, no man or woman should presume in their work to imitate the Creator.

Shisha mirror being attached using blanket stitch

4
Bead embroidery

Before embarking on an embroidery project it is best to consider carefully the materials and equipment you will need. Thorough preparation at this stage will enable the work to be carried out more smoothly.

Needles

As bead holes tend to vary enormously in size, great care must be taken when planning a project. If the hole is too narrow for even the finest needle, a wire needle threader might be useful in drawing through the working thread. In the past workers faced with this problem would fold a single human hair to serve the same purpose.

If all else fails, it may be possible to wet the thread and guide it through the hole unaided.

Naturally, beads with a larger hole will present no problems. Even a regular embroidery needle can be passed through with ease.

Very fine, straight needles are required for beading. Listed below is a brief summary of the various needles available.

Milliner's or straw needles

Milliner's or straw needles are long and thin with a round eye, and, as their name suggests these are mainly used for working on hats. They are also useful for pleating and smocking work.

Beading needles

Beading needles are also very fine and straight, but have long thin eyes. Both milliner's and beading needles bend easily and this flexibility enables beads to be gathered quickly up onto the needle.

Sharps

Sharps needles are designed for general sewing work. They have a short round eye, giving additional strength, and are produced in sizes 1–12.

Betweens or quilting needles

These needles are traditionally used by professional needleworkers and tailors. They are, as their name implies, used for quilting work of all descriptions. Their shortness enables even stitching to be produced quickly. Betweens are sold in sizes ranging 4–10.

Embroidery or crewel needles

These needles are produced in the same size range as 'betweens', but have an elongated eye, which is designed to take one or more threads of stranded embroidery cotton. These needles, which are used mainly for embroidery, are usually sized 4–10.

Tapestry needles

Tapestry needles have blunted points, which enable them to slip through fabric or canvas without splitting the threads. They are used with wool or heavy embroidery cotton. Tapestry needles are sized 13–26.

Chenille needles

These needles are short and stubby, with a large eye. They were originally designed for work using chenille thread, but nowadays can be used to stitch coarse material with thick yarn. Chenille needles are sized 18–24 and it is unlikely that they would be suitable for any but the coarsest beaded project.

Darners

These very long needles with long eyes are used mainly for mending purposes with wool or heavy cotton yarn. Darners are sized 1–9.

Carpet needles

A heavy form of sharps needle, these are used for sewing rugs or carpets. They are sized 16–18.

RIGHT *A selection of materials and equipment needed for bead embroidery*

RIGHT *Black bugle beads have been used to decorate this modern evening purse and shoulder motif*

BELOW *This example of a richly embroidered panel was produced in an Indian workshop (loaned by Joel & Son Fabrics)*

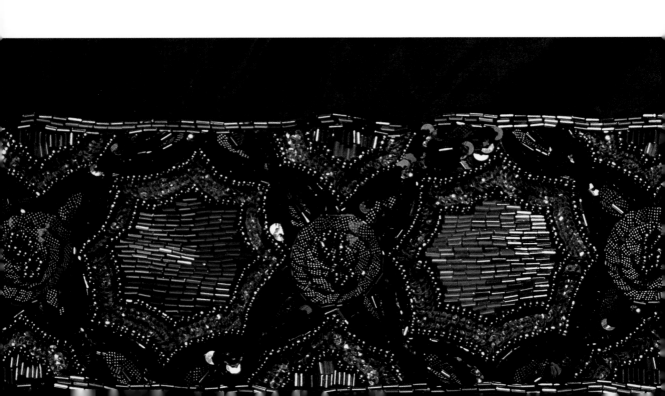

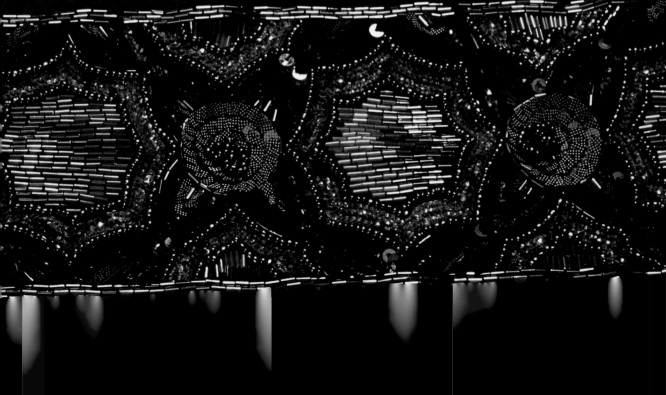

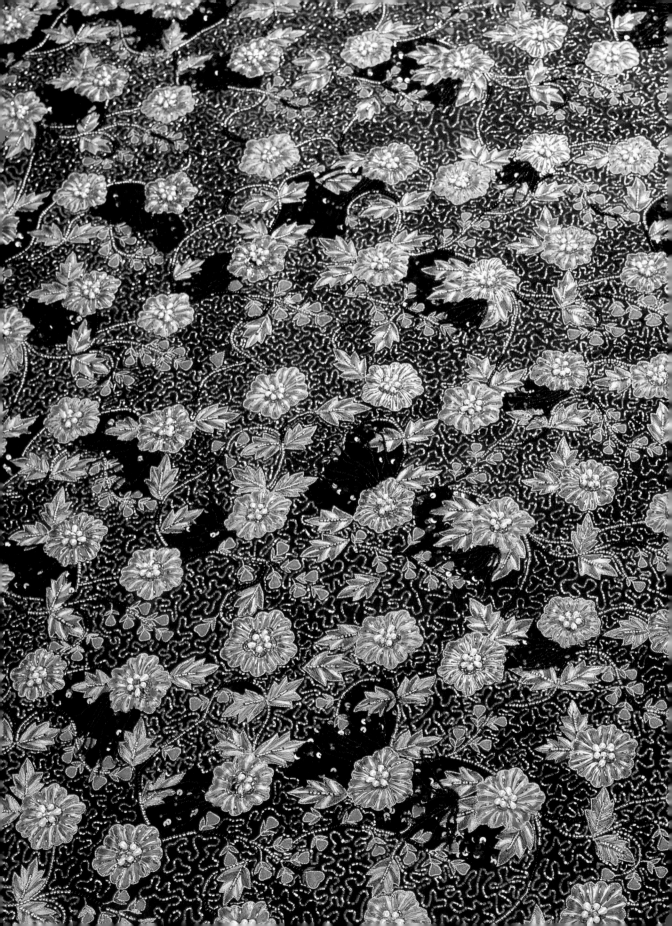

ABOVE *In Victorian times, sailors used beads to make pincushions such as this one as gifts for their loved ones at home*

LEFT *This piece of fabric from India is silk embroidery which has been highlighted by the use of beads and sequins. The free-standing flower stamens are worked with tiny black and pink rocailles (loaned by Joel & Son Fabrics)*

37

ABOVE *Berlin woolwork was often combined with beads, as can be seen in this boldly patterned late nineteenth-century teacosy*

BELOW *Goldwork embroidery has been combined with two sizes of gold beads on a stunning early twentieth-century collar*

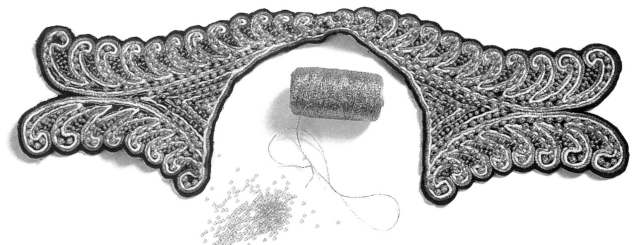

RIGHT *Lace and beads make a wonderfully dramatic impact for evening wear and motifs*

ABOVE *Small bugle and seed beads can be used to great effect on modern lace trimmings*

BELOW *A modern interpretation of an Arts and Crafts design is being worked on this collar of appliquéd silk and bead embroidery*

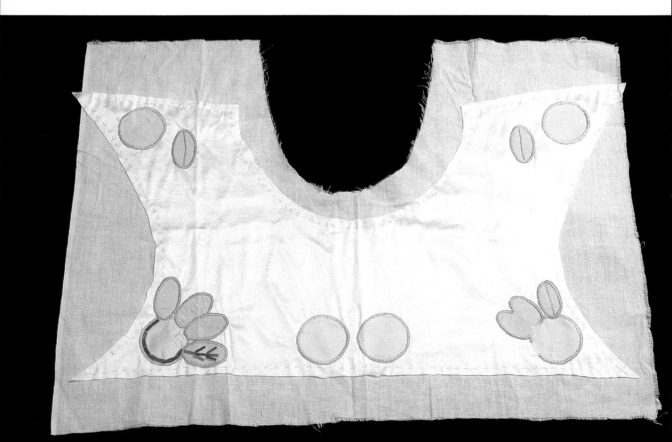

Ball-point needles

These needles were developed fairly recently for use with jersey, stretch and other synthetic materials. Their points are blunt to prevent fabrics from snagging and laddering. They are used to work needlepoint lace and for embroidering and attaching beads to knitted and crocheted textiles.

Easy threading needles

These needles are also known by the name Calyx. They have a spring at the top of the eye, into which the thread is pulled. Made especially to help disabled people who may experience difficulties in threading an ordinary needle, they are not suitable for beading, except with the largest of beads.

In addition to the above, specialist needles can also be obtained for upholstery work, mattress repair and weaving, but these would seem to be outside the scope of most beading requirements.

Thread

Beading thread is often waxed to make it stronger, enabling it to glide through the bead hole more easily. Waxing is especially important with cotton and some modern synthetic threads, which are inclined to fray.

Silk thread, which is strong and pliable, is the best choice for beading. Linen is also suitable. Cotton, however, is much more likely to break during sewing, and also when being laundered. However, whatever the choice of thread, remember that it must be fine enough when threaded to pass easily through the bead.

It is normal to match the working thread to the colour of the ground fabric or to use a neutral tone, which will blend with both the background and the embroidery. Transparent nylon thread will blend with both bead and background, but it is very slippery and, therefore, not easy to handle.

Interesting effects can be achieved if the colour of transparent beads is altered by varying the colour of the thread used to attach them. However, it is wise to experiment with these ideas on scraps of material before attempting the main piece of work.

Beads can be applied with any of the wide variety of novelty knitting yarns available, provided that their holes allow them to be threaded easily. Stunning effects can be achieved with metallic threads produced for crochet and machine embroidery. These threads are widely available in craft departments and information and materials can be obtained from the suppliers listed on pages 136–138.

Containers

It is advisable to keep all types, sizes and colours of beads separately in little plastic tubes or small glass bottles. The containers used to package photographic films are ideal for storing small beads and the multi-drawer cabinets sold in hardware shops for storing screws also make excellent bead containers. Specialist bead shops also sell a range of custom made containers.

For use, beads should be tipped into small plastic saucers, where they can be easily picked up using the beading needle. Alternatively, a few beads at a time can be tipped onto individual squares of felt. They can then be picked up from this surface with the point of the needle.

Other accessories

A pair of dressmaker's scissors and light, pointed embroidery scissors are also necessary requirements for beading projects, and these should be kept very sharp and stored safely. Scissors for needlework should be kept entirely for that purpose and never used for general craft work or to cut paper.

A well-fitting thimble is also useful and this should have well defined indentations in its surface to prevent the needle from slipping. Pins and an emery-filled pincushion, and other general sewing items such as needle threaders, tracing wheels, stitch rippers and, of course, a good quality tape measure should also be at hand, when any project is begun.

Ground fabrics

Beads can be sewn to almost any ground fabric, ranging from heavy leather to the finest of silks. They can be attached to plastic, paper and all types of hessian and canvas. The only limitation is that the chosen material must allow the needle to pass through it and be strong enough to support the weight of beads in the finished piece. Loosely-woven fabric must be firm enough to allow each bead to sit on its surface, otherwise beads may be lost to the underside of the work, which will spoil the design.

Transparent and semi-transparent fabrics such as lace or silk can be backed with nylon or cotton net, depending upon the desired effect. Cotton net is soft and will drape, whereas nylon net remains stiff even after washing. When using layers of fabric in this way, treat all layers as one. Completed beadwork can be further lined with soft- or medium-weight fabrics which will give added strength and neaten the finish.

Except for a purely experimental piece, it is wisest to keep fabric types the same throughout any project. Match silk with silk, cotton with cotton and so on. It is also a good guideline to back a fine fabric with a slightly firmer one and firm fabric with a slightly finer.

Many fabrics are given a finishing 'dressing' during manufacture. This makes them feel stiff. This dressing can be washed away before use, although the stiffness can help give embroidery a more even tension whilst working.

Frames

In order to produce good quality beaded embroidery, it is necessary, as with other forms of embroidery, to work on a frame. A well-framed fabric enables the needleworker to work regularly, and so the time and effort initially required will more than adequately be repaid.

As a general rule, small motifs are best worked in a ring or tambour frame, while larger pieces require a rectangular, square or slate frame.

Ring or tambour frames

A ring frame consists of two wooden rings, which fit together, the one inside the other. The outer ring has a screw fitting which can be tightened, enabling the fabric to be held firmly in place.

Ring frames are available in many sizes, from 10 cm (4 in) to 38 cm (15 in) and can be hand-held or mounted on a stand, which leaves both hands free for working. This is particularly essential when embroidering or tambouring with beads.

Setting up a ring frame

1　Bind or hem the fabric to be worked to prevent fraying. Masking tape can be used to bind raw edges quickly and easily.

2　Separate the two rings of the frame and centralize the fabric to be worked over the smaller ring.

3　Fit the larger ring over the fabric and tighten the screw until the fabric is loosely held.

4　Pull the fabric gently out from beneath the ring, straightening the grain within the frame as the tension screw is tightened further.

5　Continue to tighten this screw, pulling the fabric gently from time to time to obtain an even and firm tension.

6　When the fabric is sufficiently stretched, use a screwdriver to tighten the screw a little further, holding the fabric securely.

It is advisable to bind the inner ring of the frame with bias or twill binding before assembly. This will hold the fabric more firmly in place and should prevent the need to re-stretch and tighten the beading whilst work is in progress.

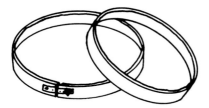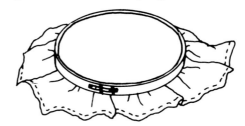

Setting up a ring frame

Rectangular, square or slate frames

These wooden frames are composed of two top bars or rollers, with tapes attached, and two flat side pieces. The top rollers or bars slot into the side sections and are held in place by metal pegs or butterfly screw attachments. Sizes of these frames vary and they are sold by tape length. They range from 30 cm (12 in) to 68 cm (27 in). As a general rule, rectangular or square frames are held by butterfly screws, while slate frames are held by pegs.

Setting up a rectangular, square or slate frame

1   When calculating the amount of fabric required, it is necessary to allow at least an extra 2.5 cm (1 in) on all sides.

2   Baste the top and bottom edges of the fabric with a single hem and oversew each side with 2.5 cm (1 in) of strong tape. Alternatively use masking tape to bind all raw edges.

3   Dismantle the frame and mark the centre point of the top and bottom tapes and the fabric with basting stitches.

4   Matching these centre points, and working from the middle outwards, oversew the top and bottom edges of the fabric to the roller tapes, with strong thread and short straight stitches.

5   Fit the rollers or bars back into the side slots, replace the pegs or butterfly screws and tighten the rollers until the fabric is taut. Further tighten the butterfly screws until the rollers are securely held and will not slip.

6   Thread a darning needle with strong thread and lace the side edges firmly back and forth round the side pieces of the frame.

7   Oversew several times at each end of the fabric to secure, wrapping the thread round the rollers before finishing.

These lacings should be tightened occasionally in order to keep the work taut.

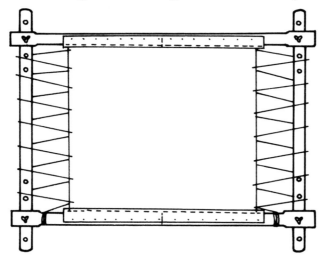

Setting up a rectangular frame

Transferring a design

When planning a beaded project, as with any other needlework venture, you will need to transfer the design from paper to fabric. In this section, the methods are explained which should enable the right choice to be made to obtain the best results.

Ideas for designs can be taken from many sources: fabrics, old examples of beadwork, modern art, sea shells, etc. It is a good idea to keep a large notebook in which to jot down ideas and to keep postcards, magazine cuttings, etc. which will be an inspirational guide when planning new designs.

The best method for transferring a design to fabric has been a problem which has vexed needleworkers for centuries. By examining incomplete work from the seventeenth and eighteenth centuries, it appears that this operation was mostly undertaken by professional pattern drawers.

The lines drawn on early fabrics are usually very fine and have few mistakes or alterations, which possibly indicates that they were always produced by professionals.

Iron-on transfers

These transfers first appeared in 1875, the invention of a firm called William Briggs, which is still in production today. They were an immediate success and were widely used in the early part of this century. Transfers do produce a very well-defined outline, which is easy to follow and which will disappear when the fabric is washed. These transfers are particularly useful for motifs and monograms. Some needleworkers feel that many of the designs are rather stilted and formal.

Running stitches

A design can be drawn onto tissue paper, which is then tacked to the fabric to be worked. The design is then worked over with small running stitches through both tissue paper and fabric. When the stitching is completed, the tissue paper is pulled away and the running stitches show the outline of the design.

Prick and pounce

This is a very old method of transferring, which is still considered accurate and effective today. Once the design has been decided, it should be drawn out onto heavy tracing paper or graph paper. The paper should then be securely pinned to a cork board and the outline pricked with a needle to perforate the paper. When the outline is completed, the paper should be pinned over the fabric to be marked and a fine powder or 'pounce' such as powdered charcoal (for light fabrics) or french chalk or powdered cuttlefish (for dark fabrics) should be rubbed and patted over the paper with a pad of fabric or cotton. Make sure that the powder penetrates the holes and marks the material, outlining the design. The tracing paper should then be removed carefully and the design painted in, using watercolour paints and a fine brush. Any excess pounce can then be blown away.

Tracing wheel and dressmaker's carbon

A tracing wheel is a small-toothed metal wheel set into a wooden or plastic handle. It is used with dressmarker's carbon paper to transfer designs or marks onto fabric. The ink on office carbon paper will not wash out of fabric and is unsuitable for this purpose. Dressmaker's carbon is produced in a variety of colours. Blue is for light coloured fabrics and white or yellow for dark materials. It is almost impossible to remove carbon from some delicate fabrics, so it is essential to test these before using.

Pin out the fabric to be marked and place over it a sheet of dressmaker's carbon paper. Place the design on top of the carbon paper and run the tracing wheel over the design, using even pressure. The outline of the design is thus transferred to the fabric. Remove the carbon paper and reinforce this outline where necessary with watercolour paints and a fine brush.

Tailor's chalk

Tailor's soft grey chalk is sold in thin discs and is used for marking outlines and sewing instructions on fabric. It is also useful for drawing round templates onto dark fabrics. Tailor's chalk is easily removed and is only used for short term work, unless the outline is reinforced, as before, with watercolour paints and a fine brush.

Water-soluble marker pen

A fairly recent innovation is the water-soluble marker pen. Resembling a felt-tip pen, it contains a marking fluid which washes away completely in cold water. You must, however, whilst working a design, keep the fabric away from any source of heat, such as a radiator or even strong sunlight, as this will 'set' the design and make it impossible to wash away. When work is completed, the fabric should be rinsed in clear cold water until the pen marks have completely dissolved. Embroidery requiring pressing should not be ironed until the marks have been removed. As various manufacturers produce these pens, it is essential to follow the instructions accompanying the pen of your choice.

Tarlatan

A design can be drawn onto a piece of tarlatan (a stiff open weave muslin), which is then pinned over the fabric. The outline is painted with watercolour paint, using sufficient colour to penetrate the tarlatan and leave a clear, but fine outline on the fabric beneath.

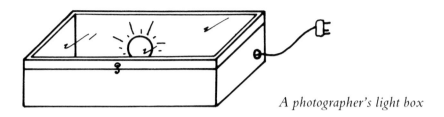

A photographer's light box

Light-box

It is possible, with materials which are light weight, to use the light from a light-box to trace a design. Place a bright electric light inside a box, and cover with a sheet of glass or perspex. The design to be traced should then be laid over the glass and covered with the fabric. Trace the outline onto the fabric using a marker pen or soft lead or white pencil.

A photographer's light-box will give excellent results.

Transfer ink

This ink can be used to reinforce the outline on a piece of fabric after pricking and pouncing or the use of a tracing wheel. It can also be used to draw a design onto tissue paper, which is then ironed over the fabric.

In the nineteenth century transfer ink was made from spirits of wine, coloured with indigo and mixed with gum Arabic and sugar. Today a satisfactory recipe is made from equal parts of Reckitt's blue and caster sugar, dissolved in a little water to make a smooth paste.

Transfer pencil

A transfer pencil is a heat-sensitive, indelible pencil used to transfer designs from the wrong side of tracing paper onto fabric. When the design has been traced onto the paper, the paper should be turned over and the outline retraced with the transfer pencil. The tracing paper should then be laid retraced side down on the fabric and the design ironed off with a medium to hot iron.

Freehand design

It is, of course, possible to draw a design directly onto the fabric with a soft lead pencil, white dressmarker's marker, marker pen, etc. In the case of modern experimental work, it is well worth trying this method, as it often produces surprisingly good results – even from the least artistic of needleworkers. Practise drawing traditional subjects such as waves, trees, flowers and shells and look around for added inspiration in magazines, art books and museums.

Sewing beads to fabrics

Before beginning to work there are basic rules for embroidery which should always be followed:

Never break a thread, always cut with sharp scissors.

Do not thread the needle with too much yarn. A long thread is more likely to tangle or knot and will eventually fray during use.

Always finish off very securely. Take the thread through the back of the material and make several back stitches, before cutting off.

Particularly when working with fine or delicate fabric, wash hands thoroughly before starting. When not in use work should be stored wrapped in a clean linen tea towel.

Very delicate work can also be protected with sheets of acid-free tissue paper. This can also be used to cover areas already worked on a large project and to wrap finished pieces until required.

Tissue paper can be used under very flimsy fabrics to add 'body' whilst working.

Fastening on

1 Use pre-waxed thread or wax a length of thread approximately 40 cm (15 in) long by drawing it through a block of beeswax.

2 Thread this into a round-eyed 'beading' or 'straw' needle, having first checked that this will fit through the holes of any beads to be used.

3 Tie a knot at the end of the thread.

4 Take the needle from the front of the fabric to the back, and make two tiny back stitches in the same place. (In this way the knot will be hidden by the first bead, or it can be cut off when the work is completed.)

5 Beads can now be applied by one of the methods given below.

Attaching round beads

1 Pick up a bead from the saucer or felt square on the tip of the needle.

2 Slide the bead over the needle and onto the thread.

3 Judge the length of the bead and insert the needle into the fabric, so that the attached bead will lie firmly in place. (A stitch that is too long will allow the bead to move, but too short a stitch will prevent it from settling securely on the fabric.)

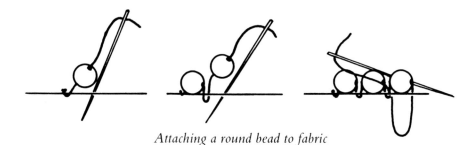

Attaching a round bead to fabric

4 At every third bead take a back stitch through the hole. This is called a 'lock stitch' and will secure the work, preventing the work from unravelling completely if the thread is snagged and broken.

Attaching a large bead with a small bead

Materials

a number of large beads
equal number of small beads, large enough not to slip through central hole of larger beads
beading needle
waxed thread
ground fabric

Method

1 Secure the thread as described on the facing page.

2 Take the thread up through the fabric.

3 Pick up a medium-sized round bead and slip this down the thread.

4 Pick up a smaller bead, take the needle through the hole in the medium bead and re-insert into the fabric.

5 Pull the thread through, settling the beads into position on the fabric.

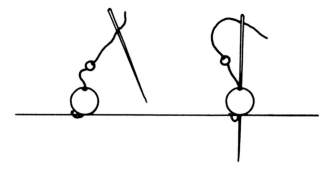

Attaching a large bead with a small bead

Flat sewn bugle beads

To sew bugles singly to the fabric, use either of the two methods described below.

Materials

selection of bugle beads
beading needle
waxed thread
ground fabric

Method 1

1 Fasten on thread and bring to the right side of the work.

2 Thread the first bugle bead and push down against the fabric horizontally and to the right.

3 Take needle through the fabric to the back of the work, a bugle bead length from the starting point.

4 Take a long straight stitch two bugle beads in width horizontally to the left, bringing the needle through the fabric to the front of the work.

5 Repeat as necessary.

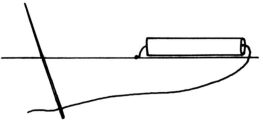
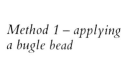

Method 1 – applying a bugle bead

Method 2

1 Fasten the thread to the fabric.

2 Thread a bugle bead onto the needle, slipping it down the thread to sit against the fabric.

3 Re-insert the needle into the fabric at the same point.

4 Make a straight stitch the length of the bead in the direction in which it will lie, at the back of the fabric.

5 Insert the point of the needle back through the bugle bead.

6 Pull the thread through and settle the bugle in place.

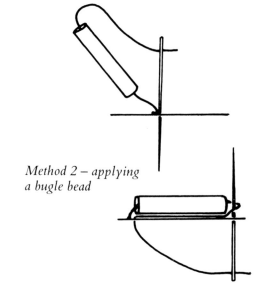

Method 2 – applying a bugle bead

7 Take the needle back through the fabric and return across the back of work, bringing it through in position for placing next bugle bead.

Care must be taken when planning the direction of bugle beads as this will form part of the overall design. Flat bugles can look particularly attractive combined with toning or contrasting sequins.

Upright sewn bugles

Bugles can look most attractive when made to stand on end. To achieve this they must be combined with small rocaille beads.

Materials

bugle beads
equal number of toning or contrasting rocaille beads
beading needle
waxed thread
ground fabric

Method

1 Attach the thread to the fabric with a knot.

2 Take thread through the bugle, then through a small rocaille bead and back down through the bugle again.

3 Pass the needle through the fabric in the same place to secure.

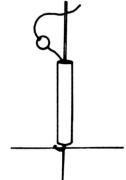

Upright sewn bugle bead

These upright bugles can look very decorative when sewn in clusters with toning or contrasting rocaille beads. For evening wear silver and gold rocailles can add to the dramatic effect.

Heavy crystal beads

Heavy crystal beads are best sewn down with a small rocaille or round bead at either side. These will prevent the sewing thread being severed by the sharp facets of the crystal and will give a neat and attractive appearance.

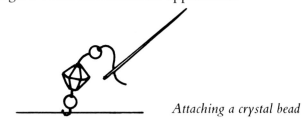

Attaching a crystal bead

Drop and pendant beads

Drops and pendant beads should be attached by threading a small round bead onto the needle first. Add a second round bead before the needle is re-inserted into the fabric.

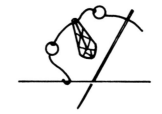

Attaching a pendant crystal bead

Finishing off

1 At the end of a row of beading make two back stitches on wrong side of work.

2 Take needle through stitching for approximately 1 cm (½ in).

3 Make two more back stitches.

4 Cut thread.

Embroidery stitches to use with beading

Beads can form an integral part of embroidery or can be applied when the work is complete. If the bead is to be worked along with the actual embroidery stitch, it will be the stitch itself which is of maximum decorative importance, rather than being seen as a means of holding the bead in position.

It is worth experimenting with various beads and stitches to find the most pleasing effects. A few of the more obvious choices are offered here, in the hope that they will offer encouragement to try more adventurous combinations.

Method of working

Slip the bead onto the embroidery thread after the needle has come through the fabric and before the final stage of the stitch is completed. Experiment with stitches and threads before beginning work on an important project.

Sequins are inclined to twist over when worked with certain embroidery stitches, so again it is important to experiment first.

Lazy squaw stitch

This quick method of attaching lengths of beads was first developed by the American Indians, from whom it derived its name. Tiny strings of beads, usually between five and nine, are laid close together and stitched in place with tiny straight stitches.

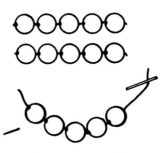

Lazy squaw stitch

Raised loops

Using the 'lazy squaw' method, raised loops can be made by sewing down strings of beads with a stitch much shorter than the stringed length.

Beads can be included with all straight stitches. Some of the many variations which are suitable are described below.

Stem stitch

This stitch can be used with beads to work stems and leaf veins in flower motifs.

Buttonhole stitch

Buttonhole stitch has many practical and decorative uses. It can be used with beads to neaten and adorn a variety of edges. Beads combined with scalloping can look particularly attractive.

Looped stitches

Beads can look very effective combined with half-looped stitches. Be careful when incorporating beads with knotted stitches, as these can appear somewhat uneven.

French knots

French knots can often be used in conjunction with rocaille and bugle beads or by themselves in rows. They can be used as stamens in flower embroidery and also as a filling stitch.

Bullion stitch

These look like an extended french knot and are worked in very much the same way. Bullion stitches can be grouped together with tiny seed beads to form 'roses'.

A rose embroidered with bullion stitches and seed beads

Chain stitch

Chain stitch is quickly worked and is effective for outlining and defining shapes. When working with beads, do not pull the links too tight.

Canvaswork: tent stitch

As the Victorian needlewoman discovered, rocaille beads can be added to a woolwork panel to add life and light. Carefully placed beads will add areas of highlight and gloss. Small beads can be sewn into position through canvas and the surface stitching using a fine, strong needle and toning tapestry thread or they can be applied at the working stage using one strand of tapestry wool and tent stitch. The beads sit neatly on the intersection of the canvas grids. All beads should be sewn in the same direction. They will face in the opposite direction to the stitch with which they are sewn.

Unless applying beads during the working stage, always sew with a strong silk, cotton or synthetic thread, which has been pre-waxed.

There are some basic rules which should be applied when working beaded canvas.

Method

Sew in rows across or in lines up the canvas, always starting each row from the same end.

1 Knot the thread, make two back stitches in the same place and bring the needle through an adjacent hole to the surface of the canvas.

2 Thread a bead onto the needle, let it slip down the thread to settle on the canvas in the correct position.

3 Make a diagonal tent stitch into the next space above and to the right.

4 Make a lock stitch (back stitch) on every third or fourth bead.

Canvaswork: cross stitch

The actual embroidery thread is used to secure the beads, which must have a large enough hole for the thread to pass through twice. Split embroidery thread can be used for this purpose.

Method

1 Knot thread and secure with two back stitches to the canvas.

2 Bring the needle to the front of the canvas at the bottom left.

3 Put the needle through the bead and allow to slip down to canvas.

4 Make the first diagonal cross stitch to the top right.

5 Repeat this procedure for each half stitch along the row.

6 Work the return row by passing the needle back from top left through the bead to bottom right as the second arm of the stitch is completed. The intersection of each stitch is secured within the bead.

Rice stitch

When working rice stitch slip two tiny beads onto each long arm of the first cross, anchoring them at each corner by taking the thread through each bead again when working the small diagonal stitches at each corner.

Small beads can be placed onto each crossed corner of rice stitch

Decorative effects

Beads can be grouped together to form repeating motifs of flowers, leaves, half-moons, or stars. Experiment with different colours, shapes and sizes to discover the most effective grouping. These can then be sewn singly or as a repeat pattern on garments, purses or as a feature of an embroidery design.

A decorative flower cluster

This simple flower motif can be used to embellish a rich design, such as the one featured on page 36.

Materials

1 large central bead
5 or more small petal beads
beading needle
waxed thread
ground fabric

A beaded flower motif

Method

1 Sew on the central bead as described on page 48.

2 Sew each of the smaller beads around this central bead.

Textured effects with large and small beads

More textured decorative effects can be made by laying strings of tiny beads over larger beads or in the spaces left between closely sewn larger beads.

Couching strung beads

This method is favoured in much ethnic beadwork. The North American Indians refer to it as 'overlaid' or 'spot' stitch. The beads are threaded in a pre-arranged colour sequence and laid across the fabric. Both thread ends are held down, while a second thread is used to couch between every second or third bead. In this manner it is possible to build up quite complicated patterns quickly and easily.

Pre-strung beads can also be pushed up the thread one at a time and attached to the fabric with a tiny couching stitch between each bead.

Achieving the right effect

In order to achieve a distinctive look on a piece of embroidered beadwork, it is necessary to use sufficient beads for the purpose.

A few beautiful beads can be used to good effect in enhancing an embroidery design, but heavily encrusted work is in a class of its own and requires skill and patience, as well as a great number of beads. Always make sure to buy enough beads to complete a particular project as supplies are often limited or erratic.

When combining beadwork with embroidery, work the embroidery first, leaving spaces for the large beads and planning the project in detail.

The larger, decorative beads should be tried in position before stitching down. Then the other smaller beads should be added, working outwards from this focal point. As with any other project, view the work from a distance from time to time assessing the design features and adapting ideas if necessary. The old advice to 'stand well back and squint' at the project may sound a little odd, but can prove invaluable in giving a balanced judgment on the design potential.

Unless the work to be undertaken is very progressive and experimental, 'objets trouvé' are best used in moderation for special effects, rather than included as an overall design feature.

Beadwork on net

Beads can be sewn to fine net using back stitch. Threads should be knotted to begin as described on page 48 and finished off with several tiny straight stitches in one place. It is essential that the beads chosen are large enough to sit on the mesh, rather than fall through.

It is also important to decide on the required finished effect provided by nylon or cotton net. Nylon net is stiff and will not drape, whereas cotton net will fall in gentle folds.

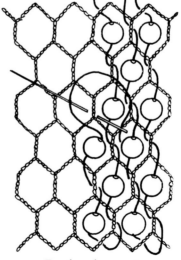

Beadwork on net

56

Large scale plastic netting can be obtained for use in experimental work for home furnishings and for theatrical use.

Beadwork on lace

Beads can be used to great effect on lace to edge outlines, to pick out the centre of a flower or to highlight certain areas. Sequins, tiny bugle beads and silk embroidery can also be added for maximum impact.

Beaded lace edgings look best when sewn with tiny seed beads and ideas for these can be found in Chapter 6.

Beadwork on fine fabrics

Spaced beading, taking the thread across the back of the work, may be used on an opaque or semi-opaque fabric. Back-stitching is necessary to hold the beads firmly in position and a net backing may be required with any beads heavier than sequins or rocailles.

Fish-scale paillettes (see page 24) can be sewn in rows across the fabric, each row overlapping the next. More beads can be added to the second layer for a very feminine and dainty effect.

The stunning beauty of shadow work embroidery can be augmented by the use of rocailles and bugle beads. The stitching and beadwork are worked onto one layer of translucent fabric, which is then covered by a second, giving a soft 'shadow' effect. When complete both layers and beads are treated as one when assembling the project.

Finishing

1 When the beading is completed, remove the work from the frame, by snipping and pulling out the straight stitches holding the fabric to the tapes.

2 Cut the lacing threads and remove.

3 Remove masking tape if used.

4 Beaded fabrics are best unwashed, but should this be necessary, use a liquid detergent and hand-warm water. Do not rub or wring, simply swish the fabric up and down in the water.

5 Rinse very thoroughly in plenty of cool clean water.

6 Place on clean towels and pull gently into shape.

7 Leave to dry naturally.

Do not tumble dry or press beaded fabrics.

5
Knitting and crocheting with beads

During the nineteenth century beaded knitting and crochet work became very popular. The beads were threaded onto the working yarn or thread beforehand and pushed up as required and knitted or crocheted with each stitch. Many beautiful beaded purses, in particular, were decorated in this way and examples of these can be seen in museums and textile collections throughout Europe and America.

In recent years, beaded knitwear and crochet work have again become popular and much experimental work has been produced, demonstrating the versatility of this combination of materials. Improved bead production techniques have led to a wider range of shapes and colours and this, together with the vast array of specialist yarns now being produced, has opened up an exciting new field to the adventurous craftworker.

It is much easier to sew beads to already knitted or crocheted fabric. The alternative method is to knit or crochet beads into the ground fabric, but this is more laborious.

Sewing on beads

Beads can be sewn on at regular intervals to coincide with indentations or focal points within the completed pattern structure. This is particularly useful on crochet fabrics. On a plain surface the beadwork may form a single design element. Beaded motifs can be placed singly or repeated at regular intervals.

However it is applied, bead embroidery should be worked in a way that will not restrict the natural give of the ground fabric. For this reason very closely beaded patterns or motifs should be restricted to small areas of the garment.

Most garments can, of course, be beaded before or after assembling. However, designs which run across seams should be beaded after making up.

Sewing threads

If the large wooden beads made for knitting are to be used, it is possible to use the actual working thread or yarn. Two or three-ply yarn can be split into single ply to pass through smaller beads. As natural yarns such as wool are not as strong as synthetic threads, cottons or linens, they can be strengthened by adding a sewing thread of a similar colour. If possible try to match materials, i.e. use cotton with cotton or wool with wool.

Small beads and sequins should be attached with a synthetic or silk thread which will tone with the colour of the project. Silk threads will, however, have more 'give' than synthetic threads and this should be borne in mind whilst working.

Needles

Where the bead size will allow, it is preferable to use a blunt ended 'tapestry' needle to work on knitwear and other stretch fabrics. Ballpoint needles are also available. These are designed especially for use on knitted fabrics, as they will not snag or pull, but slide easily between the stitches. Sharps needles may have to be used, but great care must be taken not to split the ground threads.

Method

1 Secure working thread with a back stitch on back of work.

2 Bring needle through to beading position.

3 Position bead and secure with several back stitches, taking thread through bead as many times as possible.

4 Take needle through to back of work and fasten off with several small back stitches.

5 Take needle to next beading position and repeat.

Do not run working thread too far across the back of the work, as this may cause fabric to pull. If in doubt, fasten off securely and reattach thread in new working position.

Knitting with beads

Working from a chart, the beads must be strung so that the first coloured bead to be used is strung onto the yarn last. Reading backwards from left to right across each row, the beads should then be added, until the first beaded square of the chart is reached. On large projects it is advisable to knit or crochet a given number of rows at a time. The yarn must then be cut, the next sequence of beads added and the yarn re-joined. This means that more ends must be sewn in to finish the work, but does make each section more manageable and gives an extra allowance of yarn for the working of each stitch, reducing the possibility of running out of a ball of thread, before all the beads have been used.

Method for threading beads

In most cases, the yarn will prove too thick to thread through the eye of a beading needle. The following method is, therefore, suggested.

1 Thread both ends of a short piece of sewing cotton through the eye of a beading needle, to form a small loop.

2 Pass the end of the working yarn through this loop of cotton.

3 Very carefully, push the needle through each bead and gently ease over the thread loops onto the working yarn.

4 When all the beads have been threaded in this manner, remove the sewing cotton loop and rewind the ball of working thread.

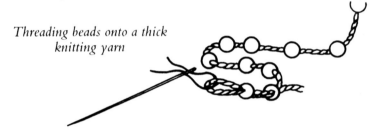

Threading beads onto a thick knitting yarn

If a great number of beads are to be used, it may be helpful to use a marker to signify the end and beginning of each row. A knot of coloured yarn is probably the best choice, but plastic paper clips or tiny pegs are also suitable.

Avoiding problems

Beads sometimes have a right and wrong way of sitting, so, if in doubt, it is always advisable to work a sample square to ascertain how they should be threaded and placed. Stitch shapes also affect how a bead will sit and these should also be checked on a sample square before beginning any project.

Beads can prove a problem when you make up a garment, so avoid beads lying too close to the selvedge of the fabric, even on closely beaded work. Leave at least one or two unbeaded stitches at each end of all rows, whether knitted or crocheted.

When beads and sequins of more than one shape are knitted or crocheted into the fabric, parts of the ground fabric will still be visible. The shape between beads should, therefore, be considered as carefully as the beads being used.

The shape of the bead, the way it is threaded, the position and direction of its hole will all affect how the bead hangs, as will the stitch used and the technique of insertion. It is always advisable to experiment with various beads, stitches and insertion techniques in order to find the best possible combination for the required garment.

To produce the closest possible beaded knitting, work in garter stitch throughout, putting a bead between each stitch on wrong side rows.

Moss stitch and stocking stitch will also give good results, particularly in patterns that require beads scattered at random across the surface of the garment.

Working beads on knitted purl stitches

Because yarn makes a loop between every two knitted purl stitches, it is relatively easy to add beads. They are pushed up the yarn, one at a time, to lie next to each previously worked stitch. This simple technique will also apply to reverse stocking stitch, garter stitch or to any pattern with two or more consecutive purl stitches on the right side of the fabric. Beads can be inserted in this way whether stitches are purled from the right side or knitted from the wrong.

When a project is planned, it is worth noting that the number of beads required for each beaded row, is always one less than the number of stitches, plus the selvedge stitches, and that a single bead cannot be centred correctly on an even number of stitches. To help a single bead sit evenly, slip the next stitch purlwise after positioning it on the fabric. For a large bead it may be necessary to slip several stitches.

Bear in mind, also that very small beads will push through openwork ground fabric and that very large beads may distort anything but the heaviest and firmest of knitting and crocheting. A little consideration and planning at an early stage, may save a great deal of disappointment with the finished garment.

Placing a bead between two purl stitches

Attaching beads with bails

Beads attached to 'bails' or little wire rings can easily be positioned between two stitches. The ring is pushed through to the back of the fabric and the bead is held in place by two purl stitches.

Method

1 Make a purl stitch.

2 Bring up the bead, placing it close against the fabric and pushing the wire ring through to the back of the work.

3 Keeping the working thread taut and the bead in position, make the next purl stitch.

Attaching a bead with a loop in knitting

Incorporating beads in knitting patterns

Stitches which are useful for bead knitting are given below and can be used with ordinary knitting patterns. However, as beading may alter tension, it is wise to work a tension square before beginning the garment.

Moss stitch

This stitch can be worked on any row or design area consisting of an uneven number of stitches.

Row 1: K1, *p1, k1, rep from * to end. Repeat this row as necessary

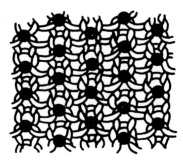

Beaded moss stitch

Plain diamonds

This is a simple pattern with which to practise beading techniques. The design is worked over nine stitches and is suitable for rows consisting of multiples of nine.

Row 1 (right side): K4, *p1, k8, rep from * to last 5 sts, p1, k4
Row 2: P3, *k3, p6, rep from * to last 6 sts, k3, p3
Row 3: K2, *p5, k4, rep from * to last 7 sts, p5, k2
Row 4: P1, *k7, p2, rep from * to last 8 sts, k7, p1
Row 5: Purl
Row 6: As Row 4
Row 7: As Row 3
Row 8: As Row 2

Repeat these eight rows as required.

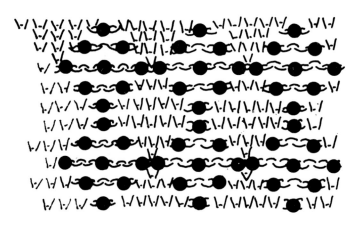

Beaded diamonds

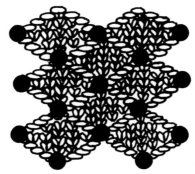

Beaded diamond brocade

Diamond brocade

This stitch is worked over multiples of eight stitches, plus one extra stitch.

Row 1 (right side): K4, ★p1, k7, rep from ★ to last 5 sts, p1, k4.
Row 2: P3, ★k1, p1, k1, p5, rep from ★ to last 6 sts, k1, p1, k1, p3
Row 3: K2, ★p1, k3, rep from ★ to last 3 sts, p1, k2
Row 4: P1, ★k1, p5, k1, p1, rep from ★ to end
Row 5: ★P1, k7, rep from ★ to last st, p1
Row 6: As Row 4
Row 7: As Row 3
Row 8: As Row 2

Repeat these eight rows as required.

All–over geometric patterns can work exceedingly well and these should be worked out on graph paper before the design is attempted. Beads can be arranged in regular patterns, such as lines, squares, diamond trellises or chevrons.

On open lacy work, beads can be used to highlight the design giving a delicate effect, and this can be further enhanced by working a beaded edging on the finished garment (see Chapter 6 – Beading trimmings and tassels).

Beads on knitted yarn-over stitches

Stitches that require 'yarn over needle' are especially suitable for the inclusion of beads. Simply bring the bead up as the yarn is put over in the normal way. When working the next row, make sure that the bead remains in position on the right side of the work.

Bead on yarn taken over needle

Beads on single knitted stitches

Single beads which are to be worked into a design can be applied in the following manner.

Method

1　Pass a crochet hook through the bead or thread a needle and cotton thread through it.

2　Carefully remove the stitch from the knitting needle and hold, either with the crochet hook or the sewing needle.

3　Draw the stitch through the bead with the crochet hook or tip of the sewing needle.

4　Replace stitch on the knitting needle and withdraw crochet hook or sewing needle.

This method of application can cause distortion. However, a small bead will cause little distortion even on quite firm material. Large beads are best kept for lacy, openwork fabric.

Pulling a single stitch through a bead using a crochet hook

Close beading

In this method of working, the beads are placed so closely together that hardly any ground fabric will show. Every stitch of every row is beaded. To ensure that these stitches are completely hidden by the covering bead, it is necessary to use twisted stocking stitch.

Close beadwork

Method

1　Thread beads onto working yarn and cast on the required number of stitches.

2　Knit two stitches.

3　Put tip of right-hand needle through back of loop of next stitch.

4　Bring up first bead to lie against last stitch on right-hand needle.

5　Take working yarn round tip of right-hand needle from back.

6 Draw loop through, thus making first beaded, twisted stitch.

7 Repeat as required to end of first row, leaving last two stitches unbeaded.

8 Continue as row one, substituting purl stitches for knit stitches on every alternate row.

Unfortunately, it is virtually impossible to keep the work straight with this type of beading and it may be necessary repeatedly to increase on one edge, and to decrease on the other, in order to minimize this distortion. However, in circular knitting this slant can be used to great effect in creating a spiral. This spiral has been used by some fashion craftworkers to create beaded necklaces and bracelets, which are quite unique.

Attaching rings

Rings can surround the stitches of a cable or other regular pattern.

Ring attached to knitted cable

Method

1 Thread a tapestry needle with a short length of yarn.

2 Slip the cable or other stitches onto the tapestry needle.

3 Pass these through the ring, so that it lies horizontally against the fabric.

4 Replace the stitches on the knitting needle and continue to work.

Crocheting with beads

Beads can be threaded onto crochet yarn, as already described on p. 60, to be worked into almost any pattern as required. The most satisfactory securing stitch is a double crochet.

Method

1 Take work to the point where the first bead is to be inserted.

2 Insert the hook into loop of previous row to work next double crochet.

Beaded crochet in progress

3 Pull loop through (two stitches on crochet hook).

4 Push bead into position against the fabric on right side of work.

5 Loop working yarn over hook and pull through both stitches.

6 Pull yarn gently to settle bead in position on fabric.

Working with sequins

Sequins should be threaded onto a doubled length of sewing thread and from there slid onto the yarn, as described on page 60. Always thread sequins so that the right side is facing the crochet hook. Cup sequins should be cup side up (concave side up).

There are two methods of working sequins into crocheted fabric, either with trebles and double crochet on non-sequin rows or with one chain loops.

Method 1

Each row must contain three times as many stitches as sequins.

1 Make a chain of the required length.

2 Make a foundation row by working a double crochet into each chain stitch. At the end of the row make three chain stitches and turn work.

3 Sequinned row: sequins are added using treble stitches. Make two treble stitches into next two double crochet.

4 Bring first sequin up and hold against the side of the crochet hook, put yarn round hook and insert into next double crochet.

5 Put yarn round hook and draw through double crochet.

6 Put yarn round hook again and draw through first two loops on hook.

7 Put yarn round hook again and draw through two remaining loops.

8 Gently pull working yarn to settle sequin in position.

9 Repeat as necessary, leaving two trebles between each sequinned stitch.

Threading sequins onto yarn cup side up

Method 2

In this case thread sequins so that the reverse side is facing upwards (convex side up).

1 Slide sequin, reverse side up, to the back of the hook.

2 Holding the sequin carefully in place, and keeping the yarn taut make a double crochet into the chain loop of the previous row.

3 Work one chain. Two or three chains may be needed to space large sequins.

4 Slide the next sequin close to the hook and double crochet into the next chain, work one chain (or more if needed).

5 Repeat to the end of the row.

Sequins placed after chain one and before the double crochet will be raised to the top of the work. This method is suitable for a garment being worked from the top down. If working from the bottom up, the sequin should be placed after the double crochet and before the chain one, so that the sequins will be positioned towards the bottom of the work.

Knitted and crocheted braids

Thin strips of knitted and crocheted fabric can be beaded and attached to the lower edges of cardigans, sweaters and jackets for decoration. These, combined with the edging techniques explained in Chapter 6, will produce stunning and entirely unique garments which will be much admired.

Large and very decorative beads can be attached to fabrics using ribbons or knitted or crocheted rouleaus.

Attaching beads to fabric using a knitted rouleau

To reinforce knitted or crocheted wear

A stretch, iron-on interfacing should be applied to the back of knitted or crocheted fabric after it has been beaded to give added support. The same applies to purchased jersey or other knitted fabrics, as these are manufactured on the same principles as hand-knitted garments and are prone to stretch and give in a similar way. This method of reinforcing can only be used on fabrics beaded with durable, unbreakable beads.

Take care not to overpress any knitted or crocheted fabric, particularly those with beads attached. In general, it is wise not to press any beaded fabric.

Knitting or crocheting with other materials

Of course, besides including beads, many other objects can be used in a decorative manner on knitted and crocheted garments. These include curtain rings, sequins, coins, jewels and even feathers. But remember that including any object or objects will make the finished garment heavier. The more objects, naturally, the more cumbersome the work will become. Small areas, which are too heavy for the ground fabric will cause unsightly sagging and will never drape correctly.

Fragile beads should never be used on items that will be subjected to a great deal of washing and wearing, and beaded garments should almost always be dry cleaned professionally. Before embarking on a project, it is advisable to check with a reputable supplier that the chosen beads will be suitable. Many modern bead finishes will be destroyed by the cleaning process.

6
Beaded trimmings and tassels

Beads have been used to form braids, fringes, tassels and cords for many centuries and traditional methods can be used today to enhance modern needlework of all descriptions, either for furnishing or fashion purposes.

This chapter includes instructions for making a wide variety of trimmings, which can be put to many different uses.

Beadweaving

This technique produces a narrow strip of heavily beaded fabric, which is suitable for use as a braid trimming or as jewellery to form chokers, necklaces and bracelets. Beadweaving has been practised by people from all over the world.

Traditionally, beadweaving is worked on a small loom, which holds the fine warp threads slightly apart at each end. Beadweaving is always worked with an odd number of warp threads, enabling a bead to lie between each.

The technique for weaving beads on a loom is very like fabric weaving, in which the warp threads (the vertical threads), are stretched onto the loom and the weft threads (the horizontal threads) are woven backwards and forwards and in and out of the warps. However, in beadweaving, a bead is placed between each warp thread as the fabric is produced, thus producing a flat, narrow strip of beadwork. When the work is finished, there should be no warp or weft threads visible between the rows of beads.

The loom

A simple bead weaving loom could be made at home, using a strong cardboard box with notches for the warp threads made in each shorter end. Alternatively, a small wooden frame, held together with glue or nails, would be adequate for this purpose. The size of the beads to be used should govern the space between threads.

However, in order to weave long strips, a more sophisticated version is required. It is possible to buy a commercially made loom, which will enable the work to be wound onto a roller as it progresses.

Two types of loom are currently available, either in wood or metal. The metal version is usually very cheap, but both are within a reasonable price range and can be purchased from specialist bead or craft shops. The easiest version to use for a long piece of beadwork has rollers at each end, enabling the warp threads to be wound backwards and forwards quite easily. When buying a loom check that the spacers are even, as irregularity will affect the finished work.

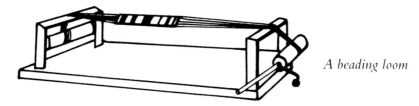

A beading loom

Threads

Strong silk, linen or synthetic threads should be used for loom weaving and should tone with the beads being used.

Setting up a metal loom

Method

1 Cut the required number of warp threads, i.e. the number of beads plus one. Each thread should be approximately 45 cm (18 in) longer than the finished work.

2 Lay these warp threads side by side and smooth flat. Gather each end and tie with a firm knot.

3 Place one knot of threads over the rivet, securing one of the rollers, and turn roller, winding a small amount of thread onto this. At this point spread the threads out, arranging them side by side.

4 Put the threads into the guide channels of the loom or space them evenly across the roller.

5 Secure the knot at the other end of the thread to the other roller rivet and wind on as before.

6 Adjust the tension on these rollers until the warp threads are held securely.

Obviously, beadwork of this type is limited by the width of the loom used. A large loom can have as many as thirty to forty threads, but it is, of course, perfectly possible to make several of these widths, which could then be sewn together to form a wider piece of fabric. The width of the bead loom obviously limits the width of the beadwork that can be made. Very long lengths can also be made by joining completed strips end to end.

Weaving with beads

Method

1 Set up the weaving loom with warp threads in position.

2 Thread a beading or straw needle with a length of suitable thread.

3 Join this to the loom by knotting to the outer left-hand warp thread.

4 Take up the beads required to work the first row onto the needle in the correct order and push these down onto the weft thread.

5 Pass the needle over the first left hand warp thread and under the second left hand warp thread.

6 Pull the thread and beads through to the front of the warp threads, leaving the first and second beads in position between the first three threads.

7 Push the third and fourth beads into position, laying the weft thread over the third warp thread and taking the needle and the remaining beads through to the back of the work.

8 Continue placing beads and weaving weft thread to end of first row.

9 Wind the weft thread round right hand warp thread, and push the row of beads to the top of the loom.

10 Repeat the above instructions, working from right to left, with the beads threaded in the right order.

In order to wind on the beading in progress, loosen the screws at the sides of the rollers and turn, moving the beadwork up. It is not essential to put the warp threads back into the guidelines from this point as the beads themselves will act as separators.

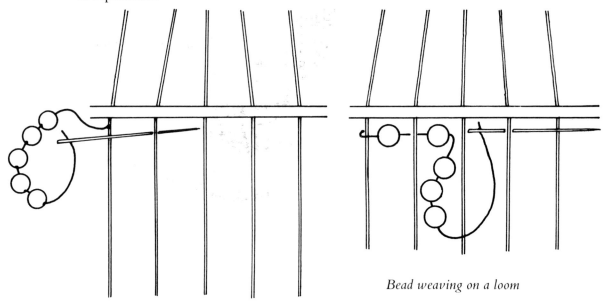

Bead weaving on a loom

When the work is finished, remove the beaded strip from the loom. Cut off the knots at each end and, using a fine needle, weave the warp ends into the bead and weft threads.

Beaded needleweaving

Beadweaving on fabric has been used for many years, particularly in combination with embroidery and drawn threadwork. It can also be incorporated into needlelace techniques to produce rich and dramatic experimental effects, as well as the more traditional uses of the past.

Beadweaving is most successful when worked on a soft, evenweave fabric such as lightweight linen or hessian.

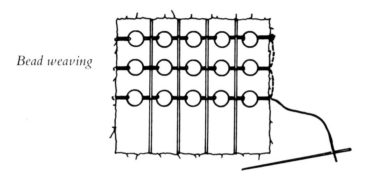

Bead weaving

Method

1 Having planned the design, mark the areas where threads are to be withdrawn with a marker pen or dressmaker's carbon.

2 Reinforce these lines with small running stitches, using sewing cotton and a sharps needle.

3 Using a small pair of very sharp embroidery scissors, cut through the weft threads on the central line of this area. On no account must the warp threads be cut.

4 Very carefully pull out the weft threads.

5 Take each weft thread back into the surrounding fabric, weaving each one over and under the warp and remaining weft threads as neatly as possible.

6 Alternatively, use tiny buttonhole stitches to hem down both sides of the design area, cutting the weft threads close to this stitching, but being careful not to cut the buttonhole stitches.

The fabric should then be placed in a frame, before the beads are woven, using the same technique described for beadweaving on a loom. For most purposes a hand-held tambour frame will be most suitable.

Woven threads are set at right angles to each other and, therefore, this type of work is most suitable for geometric patterns.

Free needleweaving

Free needleweaving

In this form of beadwork, the foundation or warp weaving threads are sewn onto a background fabric. A firm fabric is required to support the weight of the threads and beads and it is a technique that lends itself to the production of wallhangings and experimental pictures very readily.

Threads can vary in length and angle, making this type of work much freer in design than regular beadweaving. Beads can be placed on the weft threads before weaving commences, as they will ultimately be held in place by the weft threads.

This type of work should always be produced in a frame, which will hold the ground fabric at the correct and even tension. The finished work should also be stretched over a frame at the same tension before being displayed.

Needleweaving over large beads

Large beads with tiny holes or decorative items with no hole at all may be held down with free needleweaving stitches. This method is particularly suitable for applying beads to heavy and knitted fabrics.

Method

1 Decide on the position of each bead or item.

2 Using double-sided sticky tape, secure the first bead in position. (The tape can be removed after the first two or three holding stitches have been worked.)

3 Using suitable thread or yarn, hold the bead in position with a number of warp threads worked over and through the fabric.

4 Using the same, or a contrasting yarn, weave the weft threads over and under the warp threads, securing the bead and holding it safely in position.

For experimental work, objects such as mechanical parts, shells, stones, seeds or bark can be treated in a similar manner.

Strung beads

Strung beads can be attached to fabric in a variety of ways to produce decorative fringes or as an integral part of an embroidery design.

Threads

Originally, prewaxed silk was a popular thread for stringing beads. However, the most satisfactory modern thread for stringing beads is a strong synthetic, such as polyester or nylon. For heavy duty work, using large beads, monofilament nylon is the best choice. This is extremely slippery and will, therefore, not need to be waxed. It is transparent and can be used on all ground fabrics, except the most delicate.

Needles

A fine beading or straw needle is all that is required for this work. Before beginning a project, check that the needle will pass through the smallest beads. In the past, needleworkers would make their own fine needles from a short piece of thin copper wire, bending over one end with pliers to produce a flattened eye. If all else fails, this might be a possibility when threading fine beads, but the needle will need to be changed to a sharps or beading needle for attaching the strung beads to the fabric.

Method 1

1 Measure the length of a single fringe and then double or treble this length. Always use more thread than you feel is necessary.

2 Knot thread at one end with a slip knot and thread through a fine needle. To make a slip knot make a loop in the thread and take the thread end over and round this loop, bringing the thread end through the newly formed loop. Pull to secure.

3 Having decided the number of beads required for each fringe strand, thread these in the correct order.

4 Push down to sit against the knot.

5 Omitting the last bead, pass the needle back up through all the beads.

6 Hold beads in place and wrap the needle thread round the holding thread several times.

7 Pull thread tight and sew fringe in position or knot needle thread and cut.

These steps should be repeated, sewing the fringe into position as the work progresses. For maximum effect, strands should be closely sewn.

Making a slip knot

Method 2

In order to work strings of beads in their finished position on embroidery, it may be more suitable to use the following method.

1 Knot the working thread and fasten onto the fabric with two tiny back stitches.

2 Thread the beads as already explained, being sure that they are in the correct order for the finished string.

3 As in the previous technique, bring the needle round the last bead and take it up through the other beads, finishing with a buttonhole stitch.

4 Pass the needle back through the fabric in the same place as before and secure with two or more tiny back stitches, before cutting thread or moving to the next stringing position.

Decorative stringing

In order to further embellish the effect of strung beads, it is possible to use combinations of smaller beads to produce tiny loops at the end of a string. This looks particularly effective when the last bead before the loop is a bugle and the loop is composed of five or more tiny seed beads in a toning or contrasting colour. Loops work best when composed of an odd number of beads, which are threaded on after the last bead and before the thread is taken up through the string for the second time.

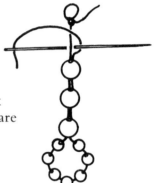

Looping a thread back to make a tiny ring

Double strings

To produce a netting or trellis effect, separate strings of beads are worked consecutively using two working threads and two needles. For a more complex design, the number of working threads can be increased, or the design can be built up two threads at a time.

Method

1 Take a length of thread three times the length of the finished net or trellis, thread through a beading needle and pass through a small glass bead.

2 Using a second needle, thread the loose end and pass both through the first large bead, one after the other.

3 Separate the threads and onto each string an even number of smaller beads.

4   Thread a large bead onto each string, followed by a further group of smaller beads.

5   Now pass both threads through a fourth large bead and repeat sequence from step 3.

6   Finish the first two rows with a large bead. Take both threads through this.

7   Take one needle through a smaller bead and let the thread hang loose.

8   Take the second needle through this smaller bead in the opposite direction.

9   Pass both threads back through the last large bead.

10   Run thread through several smaller beads on each string, turn needle and run back again to the large bead.

11   Buttonhole stitch firmly over the threads behind the last bead and tie off securely, before cutting the threads.

12   Add further strings by threading another needle, working through a small and then large bead, string a group of small beads and then pass this thread through one of the loose large beads.

13   Continue building up the net to the required width.

Loops and rings

As a single string is being made, it is possible to loop the thread back on itself and secure to form tiny rings. Variations can be made by altering the number of beads in each ring and by colour and bead changes.

Stringing beads with separating knots

Use two threads throughout as one.

Method

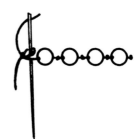

1   Thread a crewel, beading or straw needle with a double thread and make a slip knot at one end as described on page 73.

2   Slip first bead down to settle against knot.

3   Make a loose slip knot above this bead, making sure not to pull it too tightly at this stage.

*Beads strung with
separating knots*

4   Using a darning or tapestry needle, pick up the loop of the knot and carefully slide this down as close as possible to the bead.

5   When the knot is in position, remove the needle and carefully tighten the knot, making sure that it does not slip away from the bead.

6   Repeat this process as many times as necessary.

Edgings

To quickly produce a close beaded edging on a garment or project, the following method can be applied.

Method

1 Knot the working thread as before and string the number of beads required to complete the finished edging.

2 Attach to hem with tiny back stitches, using either this thread or a second working thread. Using a second thread may prove safer, reducing the likelihood of snagging.

3 Lay the strung beads close to the hem and couch into position between every two or three beads until the end of the hem is reached.

4 Fasten off firmly using tiny back stitches.

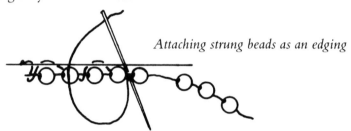

Attaching strung beads as an edging

Loops and points

By varying the bead combinations, this simple method can be used to produce many different edging effects.

Method

1 Secure the thread with back stitches to one end of the hem.

2 Thread on the first group of beads needed to form a loop.

3 Attach these to the hem using oversewing stitches placed at a shorter distance from the starting point than the length of the string of beads. The size of the loop can be regulated by this distance – the closer the stitching, the longer the loop.

4 Continue to work in this manner, threading each loop and attaching, until the hem is complete.

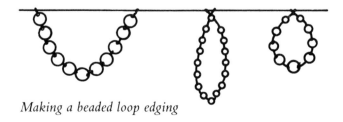

Making a beaded loop edging

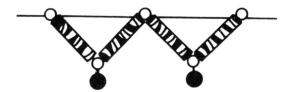

Making a beaded point edging

A combination of bugle and seed beads will give a pointed edging, while tiny seed beads will produce loops. Experiment with various combinations to obtain the best effect before beginning to sew.

Loops and points can be used across the surface of fabric and embroidery to add design detail and draw attention to particular features.

Tassels

Decorative tassels can be used to adorn evening purses and bags, belts and even dresses, as well as cushions, curtain tie-backs and embroidery.

Straight tassels

1 Make several short strings of beads and secure the working threads to a piece of masking tape, ensuring that all strings are positioned at the same length.

2 Place a folded cord, loop or other chosen fastening at one end of the tape.

3 Roll up the tape carefully enclosing the top of the threads and the ends of the cord, loop, etc.

4 Using strong thread sew through the tape several times.

5 Using strong thread, wrap and bind the tape firmly.

6 When the whole tassel is as secure as possible, make several more short strings of tiny beads and couch these round or over the head of the tassel until completely covered. Alternatively, tiny beads can be sewn on individually, until the head is covered.

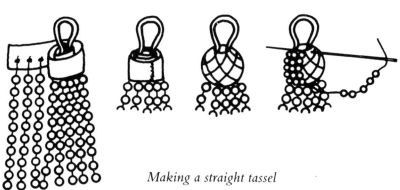

Making a straight tassel

Making a looped tassel

Looped tassels

A looped tassel is made by sewing loops of beads onto a length of tape, which is then rolled and covered in the same manner as described on page 77.

Braids

Beads can be sewn to commercially made braid to pick out the design, or can be incorporated into knitted or crocheted edgings to be used in the same manner. Beads to be used in this way should be applied before the braid is attached to the fabric.

Beads can also be used with ribbons of all widths, either as a decorative edging or to hold folds and pleats in place.

Very narrow ribbon can be threaded through large bead holes and the whole can then be couched or oversewn in position. Ribbon used in this way can also be knotted or tied in a bow round the bead for use in a variety of applications.

7
Tambour beading

A short history of tambour work

Tambour work is a technique which involves using a fine hook to work chain stitches onto fabric. It was first developed by the Chinese many centuries ago. However, nowadays India is the country most associated with this craft.

This form of chain stitching, combined with the use of tiny mirrors (known as shisha mirror work), has been a popular form of embroidery in Sind and Baluchistan provinces for countless generations. Originally, such work was performed by men. They can still be seen sitting cross-legged on the ground, supporting their tambour frame with their knees as they work. Today teams of women are also employed tambouring luxury fabrics for export.

The Indians of Peru also work this coarse chain embroidery, but their work is produced without the use of a frame. With practice and skill it is possible to manipulate the ground fabric in such a way that a frame is not required. However, for general purposes, it is essential that any work be produced on well-stretched fabric in a free-standing frame.

In eighteenth-century Europe this work was known as 'tambouring', named after the drum-shaped frame on which it was originally worked. Tambouring was considered a most suitable occupation for well brought up European ladies, allowing them to display their hands to their best advantage as they worked. The fine muslins manufactured at this time provided a very suitable background for chain stitch embroidery and its popularity developed and was sustained in the drawing rooms of the wealthy.

As fashions changed and new styles evolved, heavily beaded clothing became 'de rigueur'. Tambour work had always been recognised as a very speedy method of embroidering onto fabric, but in the late nineteenth century, Louis Ferry (a workroom manager in Lunéville, France) realised that it could also be a very efficient means of attaching beads to clothing. The technique soon gained recognition in the trade and is still used today for fashion garments and all 'haute couture' work.

Much of this early work was done by women in their own homes. They and the professional beaders in the workrooms toiled long hours for very little pay.

The problems of the workers at this time were as bad in America as in Europe and the workers who emigrated to Australia and New Zealand, in search of better times, fared no better.

Tambour beading was to reach its heyday in the 1920s, when it adorned the 'flapper dresses' of the bright young things. Not only was the entire surface of a garment covered with beads and sequins, but free-hanging tassels and belts gave added weight to garments already loaded with glitter. Small purses and evening bags were also given added sparkle and the bead industry boomed.

Today, the manufacture and availability of lighter beads and sequins has meant that beading is enjoying a fashion revival. Designers, looking to the past for their inspiration, are able to produce much more subtle and fluid effects. The technique of tambouring itself is very simple and, once mastered, proves to be extremely quick and versatile.

Round beads, bugle beads and sequins are all suitable for this method of application, the size and weight used depending upon the background fabric, the size of the hook and the type of thread.

Marking out the design

Beads applied by tambouring are attached to the underside of the fabric as it is placed in the frame. The right side of the finished fabric will, therefore, face downwards whilst being worked. The design guidelines from which to work should be drawn onto the reverse of the fabric, either with a medium lead pencil or a dressmaker's crayon.

Net embroidery can be worked over a paper pattern placed below the work. The hook is passed through the net and the paper and this can be torn away when the design is completed.

Materials

Hooks and needles

The tambour hook consists of a holder or handle and the hook (or needle) itself. Tambouring hooks are very sharp and great care must be taken to store them safely. Use a small piece of expanded polystyrene or cork in which to insert the head of the hook at all times when not in use. The hook is inserted into the holder and held in place by the tightening of a small thumb screw. Old holders may have different methods of securing the hook and often contained a screw-off cap at the other end of the handle for storing spare hooks.

Tambour hooks come in four sizes. They are made from the needles used in the embroidery trade for the Cornely chain stitch machine. The two finer sizes are for use with delicate fabrics. The medium is mostly used to apply embroidery silks and cottons, while the thicker hook is for applying tapestry wools and other thick threads. All can be used for beading and sequinning, their size being governed by the size of the hole in the beads and sequins being used.

Assembling the tambouring hook

Before beginning to work, loosen
the screw and insert the hook into
the handle. Tighten the screw
keeping the hook in this position.
Each stitch will be made in the
direction that the screw is
pointing.

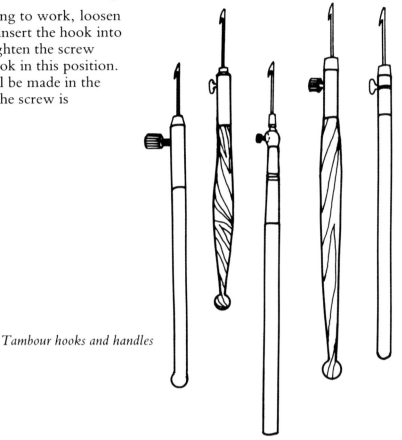

Tambour hooks and handles

Threads

Most machine embroidery or sewing threads can be used for tambour work,
although smoother thread will allow for ease of working.

It is essential that the thread, of whatever type, should be on a reel or spool,
which can then be placed on a reel-holder either to the left of the frame for right-
handed workers or to the right if you are left-handed. Alternatively, the spool
can be slipped onto a knitting needle, which can then be bound to the frame. Old
fashioned knitting wool holders can also be used and they can easily be hung on
the frame by their loops. Whatever the chosen method, it is essential that the
thread runs freely and will not pull during working. A reel holder will also, of
course, keep the working thread clean at all times.

60 denier cotton is the best choice when working with medium weight beads
and sequins. As with any form of beading the yarn should be in a colour to tone
either with the background fabric or with the beads. However, a fine metallic
thread can look most effective, when used with the beads or for chain stitch
embroidery. Do try tambouring the chosen thread first on a simple square of
fabric, as many synthetics will fray and split quite easily and are, therefore,
unsuitable for this form of work.

Beads and sequins

For tambouring work, beads and sequins are best purchased ready strung. Beads bought loose must first be threaded onto the working thread before tambouring starts. Unless otherwise stated in the instructions, sequins should be threaded face or shiny side downwards, so that they will sit right side up on the fabric.

Beads that are ready strung can be easily transferred to the working thread, by following these instructions.

Method

1 Tie the free end of the bead thread loosely into a slip knot (see page 73 for instructions) and pass the end of the working thread through this knot.

2 Tighten the slip knot securely, firmly anchoring the bead thread.

3 Carefully pass the beads one at a time over the knot and down onto the working thread.

4 When all the beads have been transferred, loosely rewind the working thread round the reel. Cut off the bead thread and slip knot. Do be sure to anchor the end of the working thread securely to avoid losing the threaded beads.

It is advisable to transfer beads over a deep box or tray which will catch them should an accident occur. Threaded sequins can be transferred in a similar manner.

Passing the end of the working thread through the bead thread knot

Tambour frames

The original type of wooden circular tambour frame was supported from below by two horseshoe-shaped hoops set at right angles to each other and fastened in the middle. This gave the worker access beneath the embroidery, which was stretched across the top of the frame and held in place by a leather strap.

An Indian tambour frame

Rectangular or slate frames

These can be used, in conjunction with a floor stand, for working large areas of fabric. The material must be thoroughly stretched, however, to provide a firm surface on which to work. The stretched fabric should sound like a drum when it is rapped lightly with the knuckles.

When a fine fabric is being used, the sides should be reinforced with calico.

Method

1 Measure the sides of the working fabric.

2 Cut four strips of calico adding 5 cm (2 in) to these measurements.

3 Sew these strips of calico to the sides of the fabric, using close running stitches and a strong thread.

4 The calico should then be attached to the top and bottom tapes of the frame in the usual manner.

5 Lace the calico to the frame sides by lapping flat tape round the side pieces at intervals, as described on page 44.

Any excess fabric should be wound round the top and bottom rollers and the work moved up and down as the work progresses.

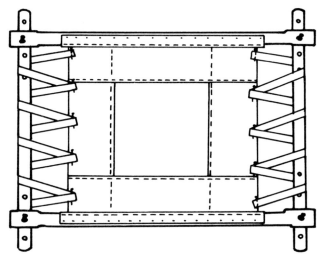

Calico-edged fabric stretched on a rectangular frame

Circular frames

These should be free-standing, either on a table clamp or a floor stand. Before assembling, the inner ring should be bound with twill binding to prevent the fabric from slipping. With the fabric in position, the outer ring should be tightened – use a screwdriver to turn the screw as tightly as possible. As the ring is tightened, the fabric should be pulled from time to time to keep it taut.

If framing fine fabric, tack it to calico which has already been stretched in the ring frame.

Method

1 Mount calico in a ring frame as described on page 43.

2 Centre the working fabric on the stretched calico and tack into position, using running stitches and a strong thread.

3 Turn the ring frame over and, taking care not to cut the working fabric, cut away the calico beneath the area to be worked, using fine pointed embroidery scissors. Great care must be exercised not to cut through the working fabric.

4 When the work is finished, carefully dismantle the frame, remove the working fabric and calico.

5 Snip running threads and remove finished work.

Methods of working

Do not attempt to apply any beads until the basic stitch technique has been mastered and the hook can be moved freely in any direction.

It is advisable to practise stitches on coarse cotton net, as the hook and its working thread can be clearly seen beneath the work. Practise until making a stitch becomes automatic and can be achieved smoothly. (Left-handed workers should reverse all instructions.)

Fastening on

1 Hold the end of the spool thread beneath the fabric with the finger and thumb of the left hand. (For added tension the thread can be wound round the fingers, as when working crochet.)

2 Insert the hook into the fabric, keeping the handle at right angles and the screw facing away.

3 From beneath, lay the thread over the hook (see diag. a).

4 Twist and raise the hook anti-clockwise, still maintaining its upright position, and drawing the loop through the fabric (see diag. b). It also helps to press lightly backwards with the hook shaft as the hook comes through, as this slightly enlarges the hole in the fabric.

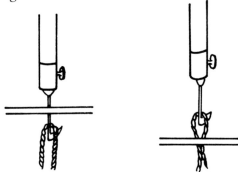

a *Laying the thread over the hook*   **b** *Drawing the loop through the fabric*

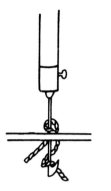 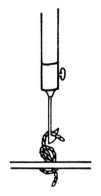

c *Picking up loose end of thread* d *Drawing the free end of thread through to surface*

5 Turn the hook so that the screw again faces away and reinsert in the same place (see diag. c).

6 Draw the loose end of thread through the first loop onto the surface of the fabric, twisting the hook again as it is raised (see diag. d).

7 Pull the free end tightly to form a knot.

8 Moving the hook slightly to the left, lay thread over hook in order to make a second small chain stitch (see diag. e).

9 You are now ready to make your first chain stitch. Insert the hook, screw facing away, into the fabric a short distance from the 'fastening on' stitches and draw through a loop (see diag. f).

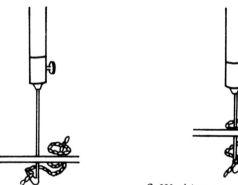

e *Move hook to left* f *Working a row of chain stitches*

Each stitch is formed in this way. Always hold the thread with the left hand using a loose and even tension or it will prove impossible to form a loop. Using this method, chain stitches can, with practice, be worked in any direction quickly and easily. The length and direction of the chain stitches can, of course, be varied to suit particular requirements, but the basic technique always remains the same.

When working a zigzag chain stitch simply change the direction of each stitch to left and right as it is worked.

Drawback stitch

This stitch can be used for attaching lines of bugle beads and rows of beads in groups.

Method

1 Use the method on page 84 to fasten on and work a first long chain stitch, making sure the hook is kept in an upright position.

2 As the hook is raised, with the left hand tighten the bottom thread. The chain stitch will slide back to the starting point. It may take some practice to achieve this result.

3 Make a second smaller chain stitch, back into the original stitch, causing it to lock and hold secure.

Finishing off

1 Make the final chain stitch of any run of tambouring slightly longer than the previous stitches (see diag. g).

2 Pull the penultimate chain stitch up onto the hook through this last stitch. Pull the bottom thread to tighten these into a knot (see diag. h).

3 Make the next chain in the same place through the fabric (see diag. i).

4 Draw previous chain through to surface and pull tight (see diag. j).

5 Finally, pull the final loop through to the surface and cut off. Pull to settle the knot and tighten thread (see diag. k).

A much easier, but not so traditional method is simply to cut and sew in the working thread, but great care must be taken to secure the final chain stitch with a pin whilst sewing in, as tambouring stitches can unravel alarmingly quickly.

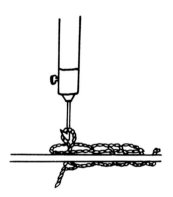

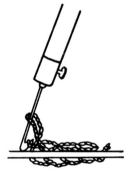

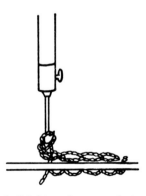

g *Making a longer chain stitch*

h *Picking up the penultimate chain stitch through the last stitch*

i *Making the next chain stitch in the same place as the last stitch*

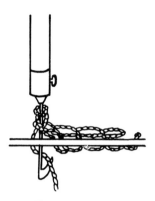
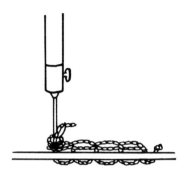
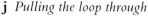

j *Pulling the loop through*

k *Cut the working thread and pull cut end through to tighten the knot*

Method

1 Anchor the final chain stitch with a dressmaker's pin, attaching it firmly to the fabric. Failure to do this may result in all the work unravelling very quickly.

2 Cut the working thread approximately 30 cm (12 in) from the fabric.

3 Turn over frame, thread a sharps needle and darn in the end very carefully, finishing with a few very tiny back stitches in a position which will not show on front of work.

4 Snip loose end of thread close to stitches and remove dressmaker's pin.

Tambouring with beads

Once the skill is learned, tambouring with beads and sequins is a very quick and efficient means of production. The beads are threaded onto the working thread and pushed up close to the fabric from below, one at a time. The tambouring chain stitch is formed from the thread between two beads.

By making each stitch the length of the bead or bugle, these can be made to lie firmly, flat against the fabric. Hold each bead to be worked between the first finger and thumb of the left hand, while making a chain stitch. Release the bead as the stitch is formed. A number of beads can be held ready for use in the palm of the left hand.

When a group of strung beads is attached, each chain stitch should be the same length as the group. If the length of the stitch is altered, the beads can be made to hang in loops or stand away from the fabric.

Small groups of beads or single bugle beads can also be attached using zigzag chain stitches. Make a single small anchoring chain at the end of each beaded zigzag to secure the row.

Applying sequins

Sequins with a hole in the middle can be attached with a chain stitch that is only half the width of the sequin, so that they overlap one another. This method is referred to as 'scaled' or 'lapped' sequins. Scaled sequins should be overlapped downwards when worked in vertical lines.

Lapped sequins sewn in circles or spirals can look very decorative. They will sparkle and reflect the light in many directions, drawing the eye to design features or motifs.

Sequins can be made to stand up if they are placed between slightly spaced beads.

Sequins can also be attached with zigzag chain or included in the upright of the drawback stitch (see page 86). After the first sequin is placed, the horizontal part of the drawback stitch is worked the width of a sequin apart. This allows the sequins to overlap just under halfway.

Attaching sequins to lie flat

1 Transfer the strung sequins to the working thread in the same manner as described for beads, but always making sure that the sequins face downwards.

2 Fasten on as described on page 84.

3 Make a drawback stitch the radius of the sequin.

4 Push the sequin flat against the fabric.

5 Make a chain stitch in the same place as the drawback stitch to anchor the sequin in place.

6 Make another chain stitch into the central hole of the sequin and the next out to the other edge.

7 Repeat steps 3–6 for each sequin.

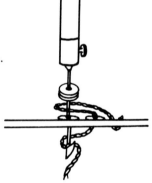

Applying sequins from right side

It is possible, with a fine tambour hook, to apply sequins with the right side of the work facing upwards. Thread sequins onto the hook and let them drop one at a time, anchoring each with a chain stitch.

Irregular sequins

These can be sewn down separately or overlapped according to the required effect. Pendant sequins and beads should always be added afterwards when the main tamboured beadwork is complete.

Irregular beads

Interest can be added to the work by the use of irregularly shaped beads, by alteration in the size of the beads and sequins and by the method of attachment. Direction also plays an important part in design work, particularly when sequins, faceted beads and bugle beads are used. Great care should be exercised in planning any project, if the maximum impact is to be achieved from the materials being used.

Fringes

As has been seen from Chapter 6, beaded fringes can add a great deal of interest and excitement to an otherwise ordinary project. Tambouring techniques allow you, with practice, to make these fringes very quickly.

Making a looped fringe

1 Having decided on the finished drop length of the fringe required, double this measurement and work out the number of beads required for each loop. String the beads onto the working thread.

2 Fasten onto fabric or hem with a small chain stitch.

3 Push up the required number of beads, until the top bead sits against the fabric.

4 Bring the beaded loop back up to the fabric and make several small chain stitches one bead-width away from the first stitch. This will make the first fringe loop.

5 Continue to repeat steps 3 and 4 for the desired number of loops.

Various combinations can be achieved by the use of different beads or by altering the spacing of the loops. On a long piece of fringing, it is wise to thread sufficient beads to complete a given number of loops. When these have been used, fasten off, thread another batch and continue working. This method has the added advantage of securing the fringing, should damage occur.

To make a single stranded fringe

1 Thread the required number of beads onto the bead thread or use ready strung beads.

2 Tie the bead thread to the working thread using a slip knot and leaving a longish double tail (approx. 2.5 cm (1 in)).

3 Slip the first bead down onto the working thread, leaving the tail end free.

4 Using the tail end of thread, make a slip knot onto the working thread and pass the required number of beads down the double thread to make the first strand. (The first bead will hold the strand in place.)

5 Cut the tail ends close to the bead and tambour the strand into position using tiny chain stitches.

6 Repeat as required, cutting thread and following steps 2–5 for each strand.

Different combinations of beads and bugles can be used to form the fringe strands. These should be threaded in the correct order beforehand. When complete each separate fringe strand should be attached along a length of tape or directly onto the fabric. It can either be sewn in position or the thread end pulled through with the tambour hook. Several chain stitches should then be worked into the fabric to anchor the strand. Finally the thread end should be pulled through the last chain and tightened to secure it.

Applying beads to net

Always make sure that the mesh of the net is fine enough to prevent small beads from dropping through. If spaced beading is to be applied, back the net with a fine fabric such as silk or organdie. This will reinforce the working fabric and prevent backing threads from showing through on the completed item.

When the beadwork is to be combined with tambour chain stitching, it will be necessary to work the chain stitching from the right side. The work will then need to be re-framed in order to work the beading from below.

8
Quilting and smocking with beads

A short history of quilting

English quilting is also known as 'wadded' or 'padded' quilting, or, historically, as 'pourpointing'.

It is a decorative form of embroidery, which developed from the need to produce warm multi-layered garments easily and cheaply. Layers of fabric are stitched together with running stitches, to produce a fabric which today can be used for a variety of household and fashion purposes. One of the oldest recorded forms of embroidered work, it was often used to produce protective garments for wear under suits of armour to prevent chafing.

In the home it has been used for bed covers, cushions and even wall-hangings.

In English quilting, the filling or 'wadding' runs continuously through the fabric, whereas Italian quilting and 'trapunto' rely for their effect on the contrast between partial padding and smooth unpadded areas.

The term 'English quilting' is, in some ways, misleading and was probably applied by early American settlers to this type of work, thus distinguishing it from the work produced in the Mediterranean and the Middle East. The peasant populations of most North European countries would have been familiar with this means of cheaply produced warm garments, often using recycled and worn blankets as wadding.

The high-fashion pinnacle of quilting came in the seventeenth and eighteenth centuries, but this was quickly lost with the advent of industrialization and the resulting flood of cheap, printed fabrics. Patchwork became a quicker, less expensive decorative domestic alternative.

Designs used in quilting have been developed over the past three hundred years, using patterns handed down through the generations. This tradition was particularly strong in Wales and the North of England. Durham and Northumberland quilts were, and still are, considered some of the finest.

In the past, pattern drawers would tour an area, marking out patterns on which the women would work. A large frame would be set up, thus enabling many quilters to work together on one item. Their chatter and gossip must have eased their work and helped pass many a happy hour. Often part of a bride's trousseau, a heart shape would be incorporated into a marriage quilt, to be used for the first time on her wedding night.

Stitches used for quilting

A simple running stitch is all that is required to produce a traditional piece of quilting. Great skill must be shown, however, in the neatness and evenness of each stitch. The beauty of this work lies in the play of light reflected from its surface and any mistakes, however small, will be noticeable.

Modern quilts can also utilize back stitch and chain stitch. Both these stitches can be used to good effect when adding beads to a design.

Beads were not applied to quilting, until quilting was used for decorative as well as functional items. The padded jerkins and doublets of the fifteenth century were often embellished with pearls and precious jewels. However, it appears that the use of beads within the quilting design is a more recent innovation.

Quilting design

As a general rule, work out a suitable quilting design on paper before beginning to work, bearing in mind the beads being used. A design is usually made up of a selection of traditional shapes which are drawn onto the fabric in a symmetrical manner. Templates can be made from stiff cardboard or bought in most craft shops. Indeed, many specialist suppliers now exist, stocking a vast range of traditional and modern templates and quilting accessories.

If a new approach is required, a look at Art Nouveau or Art Deco styles, particularly from the fashion houses of the early part of the twentieth century, may provide just the inspiration the adventurous needleworker requires and could prove the basis for a stunning new development.

Transferring the design

When making templates, the design should be traced onto greaseproof or tracing paper and then transferred to heavy weight card. It is, of course, perfectly possible, to draw directly onto card, but this needs artistic skill and a sure hand.

Once drawn, the main outline should be carefully cut out, using sharp scissors or a scalpel. Minor design lines should be marked directly onto the fabric using a marker pen or lead pencil. If these lines are complex, they can be applied using the prick and pounce method described on page 45.

The design should fill the whole of the fabric, with a main central pattern, a background or filling, and perhaps borders and corners. As a general rule designs should be kept fairly simple, as the impact of quilting relies on the spaces between the stitches, rather than the stitches themselves.

When the pattern is completed, fabric, wadding and gauze must be sandwiched together and mounted on a quilting or rectangular frame. A round quilting hoop can also be used for large pieces and this should be set up as described on page 43.

Setting up a quilting frame

1 Mark the centre point on each side of the fabric and the centre point of frame tapes.

2 Dismantle the frame and oversew the top edge of the gauze to the tape on one rail and the bottom edge to the other.

3 Reassemble the frame and push in the pegs, making sure that the fabric is held firmly, but not, at this stage, too tautly.

4 Lay the wadding on top of the gauze. The surplus should hang over the back of the frame.

5 Place the top fabric over this with the marked design uppermost. Tack along one side through all three thicknesses.

6 Smooth the top fabric over the wadding and fasten along the other side with a row of long pins. Tack carefully in position, keeping all layers smooth and flat.

7 Secure the work at either side by tying a tape round the stretcher, close to the rail.

8 Fix the tape to one corner of the work with a long pin.

9 Take the tape back around the stretcher and back to the fabric. Secure again with a pin. Continue in this way down each side of the work.

10 Tie off the tape at each lower corner.

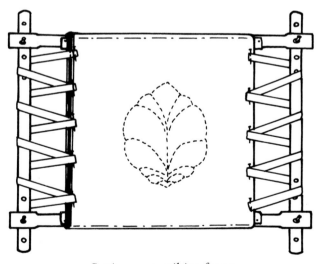

Setting up a quilting frame

To begin sewing

1 A hand-held frame can be rested against the back of a dining chair.

2 Sit comfortably at the frame and begin to work from right to left.

3 Knot the thread and bring the needle from the back to front of the work. A sharp pull will bring the knot through the gauze to sit against the wadding.

4 Work each line with a series of small, even running stitches.

5 The left hand can be used underneath the work to guide the needle.

6 Curves should be worked in smaller stitches than are used when working straight lines.

7 Finish by making a back stitch into the previous stitch and run the remaining thread through the wadding.

Running quilting stitches along working line of outline

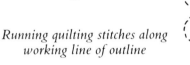

Order of work

1 Quilt the lines around the perimeter of the design first.

2 Quilt the pattern from left to right.

It may be necessary to use more than one needle, picking them up and leaving them as required. Follow the natural lines of the pattern and work towards an even sewing rhythm.

Any mistakes should be unpicked from the back of the work to prevent snagging the fabric. Quilters traditionally kept a chalk mark record of the hours spent at their frames.

When the quilt is complete, cut the tacking threads and remove from the frame. Turn the top and bottom edges to the inside and trim the wadding. Sew a line of running stitches as close to the edge as possible and another line a fraction of a centimetre away.

Machine quilting methods

A sewing machine can be used for quilting, using either of the following methods.

Using presser foot

Some machines are provided with a quilting foot which has a short upturned foot, designed for sewing over thick wadding. Some have a small guide, which slots into the rear of the foot, aiding the sewing of straight rows.

Straight stitches are most often used for quilting, but it is possible to experiment with zigzag stitches. Keep stitch lengths fairly long, otherwise fabric may jam under the foot and choose any of the more open automatic stitches or utility stitches used for blind hemming or overlocking.

Free machine quilting

A darning foot will enable free machine embroidery to be produced without stretching the work in an embroidery frame. For machine quilting, the feed teeth should be lowered or covered with a cover plate.

Sewing on beads

In general the thread used for beading should tone with the fabric background colour.

1 Fasten on with a knot on the wrong side, pulling the knot through the wadding and bringing the needle out in the correct position for attaching the first bead.

2 Make a back stitch, pick up a bead and secure with another back stitch.

3 Take the needle through the layers again, coming out in the correct position to sew the next bead.

4 Repeat as necessary.

Any method of sewing beads can, of course, be applied to beadwork on quilting.

Design ideas and applications

Quilted fabrics can give unlimited scope for the application of beads, but do not be tempted to overindulge.

The sparkle that beads and sequins provide will draw the eye to particular aspects of the design and, therefore, these areas need to be well planned beforehand.

If unsure of the required effect, try dropping a few loose beads onto the surface of the quilting, allowing them to roll and settle into the hollows. A little extra adjustment should provide the necessary balance and the beads will then be ready to be sewn into position.

As has already been seen, beads are excellent for outlining and defining important design features. Effects can be altered by varying the size, shape and colour of the beads and sequins being used. Larger, more important beads are best used as a focal point of the design, decreasing the bead size towards the outer edges of the design.

*Free standing quilted and beaded
petals and leaves*

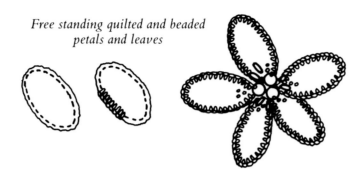

Making detached petals or leaves

These quilted and beaded petals or leaves can be made and appliquéd to blouses, cushions, evening bags, etc.

1   Draw the outline of a simple leaf or flower petal onto the prepared quilting fabric.

2   Straight stitch around this outline.

3   Cut out the shape through all layers with sharp scissors just outside the stitched line.

4   Oversew with satin stitch or blanket stitch.

5   Assemble four or five petals and stitch together, applying a cluster of small beads to the centre of the completed flower: alternatively, stitch tiny beads to vein lines of leaves or use with french knots as filling stitches.

Appliquéd petals and leaves can be seen on the collar on page 40.

Italian quilting

There are two methods of cord quilting, both of which are referred to as Italian quilting. In method one, two parallel lines of back stitch are worked round the design outline through two thicknesses of fabric. A small slit is then made in the backing fabric and a cord or thick thread is run between the lines to give a padded outline. In method two, the cord is laid down and then two lines of stitches are worked to hold this in position.

This form of decoration was popular during the Renaissance, relying as it did on the rich silks and satins which are so typical of this work. Almost any closely woven fabric can be used, however. Italian quilting wool can be used to thread between the lines of stitching, but if this is not available, almost any soft, bulky yarn can be used. The working threads must be strong. Linen is the obvious choice and to facilitate working this should be waxed before use.

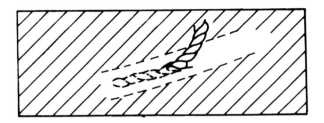

Method 1 – stitching either side of a laid cord

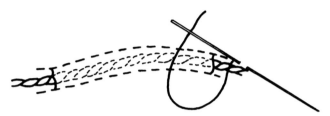

Method 2 – running a cord between two lines of stitching

As with most other forms of embroidery, a frame should be used. Transfer the design elements with a single drawn line and work rows of stitching evenly on either side of this.

Trapunto quilting

This method of quilting is also known as 'stuffed' quilting, or 'matelasse' and consists of padded areas, outlined with running stitches. The fabric traditionally used was unbleached linen.

When the stitching is completed, the stuffing can be introduced from behind through slits cut in the backing fabric. Stuffed quilting is often combined with cord quilting and surface embroidery, particularly in modern work.

Trapunto has a particularly rich appearance, containing raised areas, surrounded by flat, slightly puckered ground fabric. From this point of view, it is an ideal medium to combine with beads, which can be grouped together or scattered at random over the surface of the work.

Floral subjects have been most popular for this form of quilting, but any curved or rounded shape should work well. Variety and size are of great importance when planning an overall design.

Great care must be taken not to cut the surface fabric when slitting the backing. If the backing fabric is sufficiently loosely woven, it may be possible to produce a hole by using a stiletto, but again care must be taken not to damage the surface fabric.

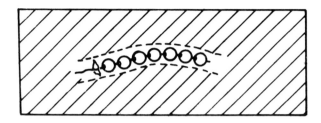

Using two layers of transparent fabric to produce shadow quilting

Shadow quilting

The technique of shadow quilting can be used on all forms of raised quilting, but it is most usually applied to Italian quilting. Coloured threads, fabric or wadding are stitched through the lining fabric to then be seen through a top layer of transparent fabric.

The stuffed areas can be outlined individually, as in trapunto work, and the wadding added. Start from the centre of the design and work outwards.

Shadow quilting can also be used in flat work and as a means of applying beads to a design, protected by a layer of sheer terylene or chiffon.

Stobbed quilting

Stobbed quilts have a continuous filling, held in place by a single knotted stitch, bead or sequin, rather than lines of stitching. Quilting of this type is sometimes referred to as 'tied' quilting.

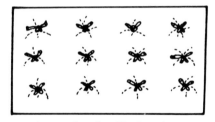

A sample of stobbed quilting

Method

1 Measure the top fabric to be used and mark dots at equal spaces across the surface, forming a grid.

2 Cut wadding and gauze and frame up the fabrics as described on page 93.

3 Use a small straight stitch to mark the position of each tie.

4 Secure each tie using a strong knotted linen thread.

5 Pull up each securing stitch very tightly to produce a dimple in the top fabric.

6 Use a large bead or cluster of beads to further define each tie if required.

The surface of the fabric could be decorated with ribbon, embroidery or appliqué before being tied.

A short history of smocking

The word smock comes from the old English word 'smoc', meaning to put on a garment. This, by popular usage, came to mean a 'shift' or 'chemise'. The word 'smock-frock', used to denote an item of clothing as we recognise it today, was first used in 1831.

Shifts were originally very plain, shirt-like garments, which soon developed into voluminous overgarment worn by labouring men, usually engaged in strenuous manual occupations.

One of the earliest examples of a pictorial record of the English smock can be seen in a painting from the time of Charles I (early seventeenth century), but, unfortunately for modern needleworkers, it is not possible to identify the stitching used on the garment.

Smocking is one of the only peasant crafts of England and was widely used in rural areas until the beginning of this century. Different areas of the country favoured different designs and colours, as can be plainly seen from the blue Sussex frocks and the black smocks of the Isle of Wight.

A well-made smock is a beautiful garment, which was always worn with pride.

The stitches used to construct and decorate a smock are very simple. They include single, double and treble feather stitch, single chain and stem stitch – all of which can be combined with beadwork for a new approach to this ancient skill. Smocking is often most effective when simply planned, however, and great care must be taken not to over decorate and thus spoil the finished effect.

Success in smocking, as with all other forms of embroidery, lies in evenness of tension and regularity of stitching.

Soft fabrics are best because the fabric must drape well and be fine enough to settle into the finished 'reeds' or 'tubes'. Original smocks were worked in evenly woven soft linen. Whatever fabric is chosen, a similar thread should be employed. A matt-finished embroidery thread was traditionally used and in general will still look more effective than a glossy modern variety.

Beaded smocking

Smocking lends itself to the inclusion of beads. Modern experimental work has led to the recognition of smocking as a form of design, instead of just a technique.

Traditional smocked garments were constructed from rectangular pattern pieces. This made cutting out the garment economical and easy. Extra fullness was controlled by gathering the fabric, which was then held in place with smocking stitches.

The stitches used were not only practical, their use brought a unique decorative quality to each garment. Patterns varied from area to area, but were not necessarily linked to the trade or occupation of the wearer, as has been suggested in the past.

Victorian needlewomen used smocking to decorate children's clothes but examples with pearls and small beads can be seen on wedding and evening dresses of the time.

To prepare material for smocking

The fabrics most suitable for smocking are spun silks, crêpe de chine, tussore, ninon, chiffon, linen, soft cottons, holland, voile, muslin and cashmere.

Any piece of smocking will require three times the finished width of material. This amount of fabric is needed for the gathering (that creates the reeds or tubes) and a seam allowance on each side of 5 cm (2 in).

Transfer dots sold for marking fabric are not recommended, as it is impossible to ensure that these dots sit accurately on the warp and weft threads of the material. This can only be achieved by careful preparation in the initial stages, as described below, but the finished results will be worth the effort involved.

Threads

Choose from twisted embroidery thread, coton à broder, perlé, soft linen thread or stranded cotton. Other finer threads may be preferred for beaded smocking. Colours which match the background fabric are usually the most effective, but gold, blue or pink can look attractive on a cream ground. Soft green fabric can look charming when worked in turquoise blue, navy in pale blue or crimson, or brown in old gold. Two or three toning colours can also be used to good effect.

Needles

For embroidery, a fine crewel embroidery needle with a long eye (numbered from 5 to 8) will accommodate the thicker threads without pulling and snagging the fabric. For feathering, a sharps 7 or 8 will prove most suitable.

Method

1 Run a tacking thread of coloured cotton down either side of the fabric, 5 cm (2 in) from each edge. The threads must be run very carefully along the warp of the material.

2 Using a marker pen or lead pencil, mark the starting and finishing point for the gathering lines down each of the coloured threads. Rows of gathers should not be more than 1.3 cm (0.5 in) apart and should begin 1.3 cm (0.5 in) from the upper edge of the material.

3 Knot a length of strong, linen thread and mark with a pencil or fabric marker the length required for the width of the finished gathering. This will enable each thread to be pulled up accurately to the required length.

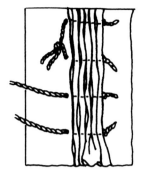

Material prepared for smocking

4 Carefully counting the number of warp threads in each stitch and working along the weft thread, run the first line of gathering stitches from right to left, anchoring with two small back stitches before starting to work. Take up a small even amount of fabric with each stitch.

5 At the end of the row, leave the thread loose, do not fasten off.

6 Remember that each line of gathering must have a separate thread.

7 When all the gathering rows have been completed, pull the threads up two at a time to their pencil marks and knot the two together firmly with a slip knot that can be reopened if necessary. Do not pull the gathers too tightly, the 'reeds' should be moveable to allow passage of the needle when you embroider.

8 Arrange all the gathers evenly before beginning to embroider.

Working the embroidery stitches

When working the embroidery, do not draw the stitches too tightly, as the work must have some 'give'. The lines of gathering will act as a guide to keep the rows of stitches straight and also in spacing the rows.

Stem stitch

This outline stitch is possibly the most frequently used stitch for working stems and leaf veins in flower motifs. It is used for starting most patterns in smocking.

Method

1 Bring the needle through from back of work on design line.

2 Hold thread down with thumb of left hand, inserting the needle a stitch length away along this line.

3 Take a small stitch backwards to the left (see illustrations overleaf).

4 Pull the thread through gently to settle the first stitch against the fabric.

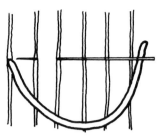
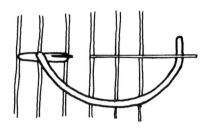

Making the first stem stitch   *Making the second stem stitch*

5 Move to the right and make the next stitch.

6 Continue to work across the reeds in this way until the row is complete.

Cable stitch

This stitch is similar to stem stitch, except that the needle is inserted horizontally and the thread is held alternately above and below the needle.

Method

1 Bring the needle through the fabric to the front of the work.

2 Hold the thread with the left thumb below the needle and work a stitch to the right (as described in stem stitch).

3 Work the next stitch along the design line in the same manner, but keep the thread above the needle.

4 Repeat alternate stitches along design line to end of row.

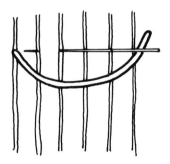
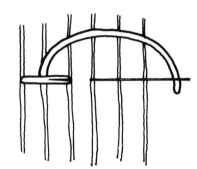

Making the first cable stitch   *Making the second stitch, keeping the thread above the needle*

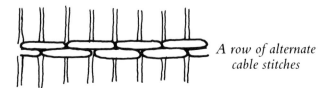

A row of alternate cable stitches

Single feather stitch

This can be thought of as a buttonhole stitch worked down a line instead of along it from left to right. Correctly executed it has an attractive feathery effect and can be combined with other embroidery stitches. It is important to keep the stitches as even as possible. For practice, it is advisable to draw two parallel lines to control the width of your stitches. With such guidelines, it will soon be possible to control the regularity of the stitching.

Method

1 Bring thread through on the second reed on the right-hand side of smocking.

2 Make a loop and hold this down with the left-hand thumb.

3 Insert the needle slightly lower down into the first reed on the right.

4 Make a diagonal stitch downwards and to the left between the two reeds, keeping the thread under the needle.

5 Pull the thread through and secure this stitch with a small vertical straight stitch.

6 Continue to make feather stitches to the right and left for the required length.

Feather stitches can be worked across smocking horizontally or vertically.

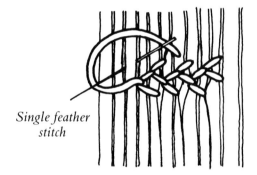

Single feather stitch

Double feather stitch

Double feather stitch

Use the same basic method as single feather stitch, but work two stitches to the right and two stitches to the left each time.

1 Bring the needle out at the top of the left hand line.

2 Working as before, make a stitch to the middle line.

3 Make the third stitch on the outer line.

4 Take the needle back to the centre line for the fourth stitch.

5 Take the needle back to the left hand line for the fifth stitch.

6 Repeat moving to left and right as required.

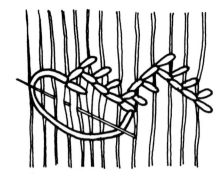

Treble feather stitch

Treble feather stitch

This stitch is worked as double feather stitch, but an extra move to left and right is included at each pattern repeat.

Chain stitch

Chain stitch is a quickly-worked and effective outline and padding stitch.

1   Begin at the top of the line and work downwards.

2   Bring the needle through from the wrong side, then put back just to the right of the starting point, but as close as possible.

3   Hold down the thread with the left thumb, to form a loop.

4   Bring the needle out a link space lower down the working line.

5   Draw the needle through and pull the thread down to form a link.

6   Hold it, as before with the left thumb, while putting the needle back just inside the link.

7   Repeat as required, keeping the thread to the left.

8   Particularly when using beads, do not pull the links too tight.

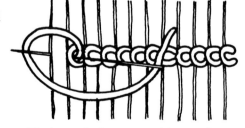

Chain worked over smocking reeds

Couched chain stitch

1   Work a row of fine chain stitches.

2   Couch with a contrasting thread, taking a beaded stitch over each link.

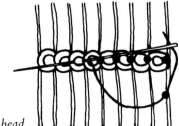

Couched chain stitch with a bead

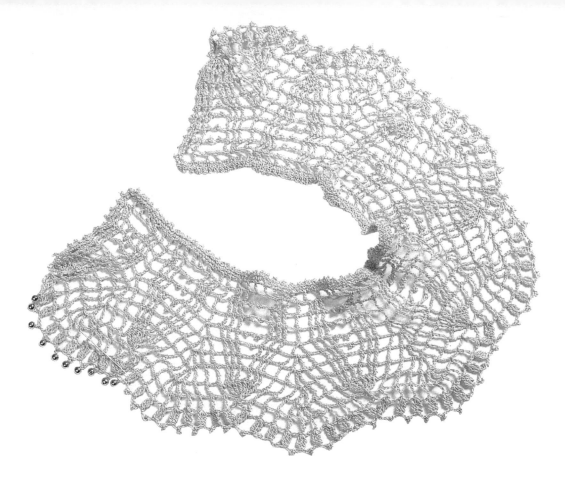

ABOVE *A crocheted collar from the 1950s can be enlivened and updated by adding beads*

BELOW *A delicate crocheted rouleau necklace of tiny beads with a flower pattern in cream and red on a brown background*

RIGHT *Beads can be added to commercially produced fringes and braids, or woven and threaded to make customized tassels and edgings*

ABOVE *An Art Deco heart-shaped motif of red, blue and bronze seed and bugle beads*

BELOW *These 1920s' chokers have been worked with the finest of rocailles*

RIGHT *Once learned, tambouring provides a quick and versatile method for applying beads and sequins*

ABOVE *A dramatic tamboured design has been combined with a simple looped fringe to produce this Art Deco evening bag*

ABOVE *This beaded net from the 1920s shows the Egyptian influence on fashion inspired by the discovery of Tutankhamen's tomb*

LEFT *Brown and cream rocaille beads were tamboured onto net to produce this purse*

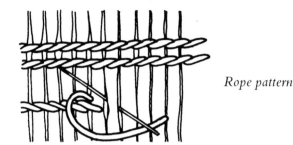

Rope pattern

Rope

This pattern consists of a line of stem stitches worked from reed to reed, each stitch taking a small section of material. The rope can be worked in single, double or treble lines of stem stitch in one direction or in alternating rows backwards and forwards.

Rope gives a very firm finish and two or three lines can be worked at the top and bottom of each piece of smocking.

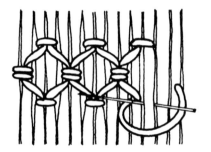

Basket pattern

Basket

The basket design is worked by two lines of rope. The thread is taken alternately to the right and left of the needle as the row is worked.

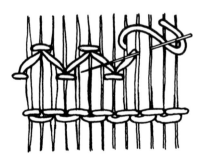

A variety of effects can be achieved by varying the grouping of the chevrons

Chevron

This pattern is worked in stepped stem stitch forming a chevron design. Care must be taken to keep the stitches at right angles to the reeds. Passing the thread to the right or left of the needle governs the direction of the chevron.

Other embroidery stitches, though not so traditional, can be used to produce distinctive designs.

When the embroidery is complete, cut the tacking stitches and remove. Well-worked, the smocking will be very elastic and, on clothing, will allow considerable movement.

Adding beads and sequins

Beads can be sewn either onto the ridges of the reeds or into the spaces between. Single beads can be sewn on to form chevron or diamond patterns. Tiny strings of beads can be looped across the design or used to accentuate outlines. These can be alternated with bugle beads or rows of sequins.

The hollows between honeycomb stitches are ideal for placing oval beads such as pearls or crystal drops. Sequins can be scattered in the hollows created by the design or tiny beads placed at intersections.

Beads applied with the working thread

Beads can be sewn on during the actual working of smocking stitches. If, however, the embroidery thread will not pass easily through the bead, one of the following methods can be adopted.

Method 1

1 Work the majority of smocking stitches first using regular embroidery thread.

2 Apply the beads, using a finer thread to work these embroidery stitches.

Method 2

1 Use a finer thread than normal to work the embroidery, attaching the beads at the same time. Thin metallic thread is ideal for this purpose.

Working method

Whichever method is chosen, the method of applying the bead is the same. Slip the bead onto the working thread as it is required and before the stitch is completed. Stitches which have long connecting threads which pass across the tubes are ideal for supporting beads.

The number of beads or sequins can be varied to suit the length of a particular stitch.

9
Design techniques

How to enlarge a design

It is often found, when planning a project, that the size of design chosen from a source, such as a postcard, photograph or original craftwork, is unsuitable for the purpose. It is useful, in these cases, to have the ability to enlarge or reduce the design by the following means.

Materials

strong, high-quality tracing paper – a piece large enough to cover the original artwork or photograph
cartridge paper – slightly larger than the finished drawing
ruler
pencils
rubber/eraser
fine felt-tip or ballpoint pen
set square
cork board

Method

1 Trace the design onto tracing paper using an HB or softer lead pencil.

2 Draw a rectangle round the traced design and divide this into 2.5 cm (1 in) squares. (A very elaborate design may need dividing into smaller squares.)

3 Number or letter each square down and across (see diag. a).

4 Tape the cartridge paper to the cork board and pin the tracing to it in the bottom left hand corner (see diag. b).

5 Draw a diagonal line from the bottom left hand corner (C), extending to the top right corner (B) of the cartridge paper (see diag. c).

6 Decide on the width of the finished diagram and draw a line across the bottom of the cartridge paper (C-D) to that width (see diag. d).

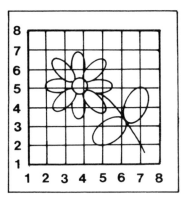

a *Dividing the traced design into a grid pattern*

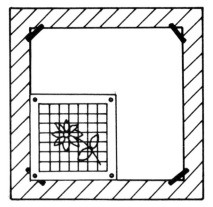

b *Pin tracing to cartridge paper*

7   Use the set square to produce a 90 degree angle, drawing a vertical line from this point to meet the long diagonal line (see diag. e).

8   Measure the height of the vertical line and extend the horizontal line C to A.

9   Draw a horizontal line from line C to A, to meet the diagonal (see diag. f).

10   Remove the tracing paper and draw in the bottom left hand corner of the rectangle.

11   Count the squares in the tracing paper rectangle and divide the large rectangle into the same number.

12   Number and letter these squares in the same way.

13   Carefully reproduce the lines of the traced design from the small squares to the large. Do this with a soft pencil, so any mistakes can be erased.

14   The same grid method can be used to reduce a large design.

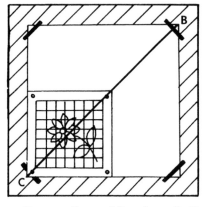

c *Draw a diagonal line from C–B*

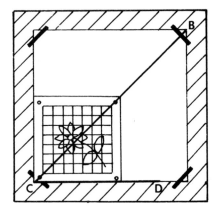

d *Extend bottom line from C–D*

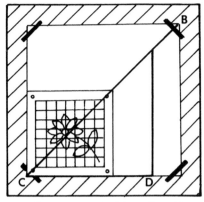 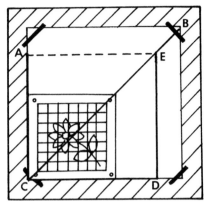

e *Draw a vertical line from D to meet the diagonal line*　　　**f** *Draw the line from C–A*

Transferring a design to fabric

When the design is complete, transfer to fabric using one of the methods described on pages 45–47.

Fabric painting

The use of fabric paint with embroidery and beading is a technique that is becoming increasingly popular, as it offers endless opportunities for experimentation.

Fabric paints are available in craft materials departments of large stores and also in art shops. These can be painted directly onto fabric with an artist's brush. The design is then 'set' with a warm iron.

Dyes and fabric paints can be watered down for use in an airbrush, and then sprayed onto fabric to give a misty, speckled effect which makes an excellent base for beading and textured stitching.

Combining beading with fabric painting

If beadwork is to be combined with fabric painting, it is essential to choose the right fabric as the basis of your design. In general a closely woven evenweave fabric, such as pure cotton, linen or silk, is most suitable. Counted thread fabrics can also be used or even curtain lining material, dress fabrics or furnishing linen. The texture of the backing material should be incorporated into the overall design effect of the project and so should be chosen accordingly.

It is also essential to take into consideration the fibre content of the fabric. Most fabric paints need to be 'set' with a hot iron and painted areas should be carefully worked out and applied before embroidery and beading takes place. This may cause a problem when working with silk fabrics and threads and it is always wise to test sample pieces before beginning to work. Whatever medium is chosen, do check and follow manufacturer's instructions in order to achieve the best possible effects.

When working with fabric paints, keep an open mind to design possibilities and don't be afraid to adapt ideas as the work develops.

Using interlinings

Bonded fabrics such as Vilene, both the iron-on and sew-in types, are suitable backing fabrics for beaded work of all types. This can either be attached to the wrong side of the working fabric to give body whilst working, or to help hold its shape when finished.

However carefully worked, even in a frame, there is a possibility that a piece of beaded embroidery may distort. A firm piece of interlining will help provide a secure base, especially if the working fabric is loosely woven or very fine.

Threads

Stranded cotton is the most obvious choice for combining embroidery with fabric painting. It is available in a wide range of colours, including shaded tones and can even be purchased in skeins which incorporate gradual shading. By differing the numbers of strands in one area, it is possible to achieve various textural effects.

Soft embroidery threads are slightly thicker than stranded cotton and are not usually divisible. The softness of these threads will produce a soft but rich texture. They are often produced in a range of subtle colours.

Coton à broder is manufactured with a high twist, producing a surface sheen which is not always apparent in other types of thread. In recent years this type of yarn has been produced in a much wider range of colours than previously existed and this has made them much more suitable for a variety of projects.

For heavier use, tapestry wool can be used. It is softer and warmer to the touch than cotton thread and the colour range is usually very wide and very subtle, enabling stunning colour combinations to be achieved.

If a very textured effect is required, it is, of course, possible to use fancy knitting and crochet yarns. These can look particularly effective when couched across a painted area interspersed with bugle beads and sequins.

Glitter threads, coiled gold wire, strips of metallic paper or fabric can all be incorporated into a futuristic or abstract design, giving endless combinations for the needleworker.

Using glue

Glue may not, at first sight, seem an appropriate choice for needlework, but it can be useful for attaching pieces of fabric and thread to a piece of appliqué work. Always use an adhesive which is colourless when dry and use very sparingly. Glue can seep out at the edges or show on the right side of the fabric.

A spray glue (glue in a pressurized can) is also useful if large areas are to be stuck down on the working surface. Use these with care, however, and always work in a well-ventilated room. The area round any design should be well protected with old newspapers to prevent a mist of glue from settling on surrounding surfaces.

Other design possibilities

Appliqué work can be an interesting addition to beaded work. Cord, lace, ribbons and braids can be included in a design, but to be effective they must form part of the overall design and not merely be an 'afterthought' or a means of using up a mistaken purchase.

Blending techniques and stitches

Each embroidery depends for its success on the sympathetic use of fabrics, colours, threads and stitches. Bold effects can be produced by the use of glossy yarns on a matt background or thick threads on a woven tweed. Do try stitches before beginning to work, this will also give an idea of how much area they will cover. Decide from these samples whether the stitches should be tightly placed, to cover the ground fabric, or widely spaced, showing the working fabric and giving a light and airy feel.

Experiment too with the sizes of stitches. A pleasing variety of different sized stitches can be grouped together to increase interest. This is particularly true of simple stitches such as satin stitch.

Stitches can also be worked at different angles to reflect the light from many surfaces, thus adding variety and impact to the work.

Appliqué

Appliqué is the technique of applying one fabric to another. These fabrics are applied to a base fabric, which can be cotton, calico, furnishing fabric, dress material – in fact almost any woven material is suitable. The choice of fabric often depends on whether any of it will show in the completed work.

It is essential that any appliquéd fabrics are carefully chosen to be similar in weight, both to each other and to the ground fabric and that fabrics be grouped together in a way which they complement each other in texture and colour.

It is wise to use fabrics that will not fray. However, if a particular fabric has been chosen, which has this tendency, it can be stabilized with iron-on, lightweight interfacing, which will add body and stability.

Cutting out shapes for appliqué

The design should be drawn out and transferred as already described. Trace each appliqué shape separately, noting which fabric is to be used and allowing a small amount for a turning hem along each edge. These pieces are then either lapped over the previous piece by this amount or the edges are turned in before being attached. As the pattern pieces are traced, it is advisable to mark in the straight grain line, so that all the finished pieces will lie in the same direction. However, for certain dramatic effects, some pieces can have the grain lines deliberately reversed.

Apply the fabrics in the correct sequence, so that the background pieces are worked first with the top layers last.

Sewing appliqué

Use a needle threaded with a strong sewing thread of a similar colour to the piece being attached. A blanket stitch or oversewing stitch can be used over the raw edge or hem, securing it to the base fabric at the same time. The distance between these stitches should be gauged by the type of material being sewn and the required effect. A very closely worked blanket or satin stitch will look particularly attractive on silks or shiny fabrics.

Blind appliqué

For materials that have a tendency to fray or are very sheer, turn a small hem on each raw edge. All edges that will show in the finished piece should be turned over and pressed on the wrong side. They can then be tacked into place on the base fabric.

When working a curved edge, make little easing cuts every so often along the curve to make turning the hem a little easier. Place each appliqué section on the base fabric and slip stitch into position using a similar coloured thread.

Quilting

Quilting and smocking can also be included with fabric painted beading and information on techniques and uses can be found in Chapter 8.

Knitting and crocheting

Knitting and crocheting can also be included in an experimental piece of work, either as the background fabric or as section to add textural interest. Stocking and garter stitches seem the most obvious choice, but a book of knitting stitches will provide endless inspiration. Close beaded knitted panels can be worked and included, and instructions for this can be found in Chapter 5.

Torn strips

Torn strips of fabric can be knotted with beads and objets trouvés to be incorporated in a design, very much in the way rag rugs are worked. Torn and knotted chiffon or silk can look particularly stunning with large decorative beads.

Finishing and mounting work

The final finishing and mounting of a piece of work is almost as important as the quality of the original design, the choice of colour and the needlework employed. Many good pieces of embroidery have been ruined by being poorly mounted.

When a piece is completed, make sure that all threads are safely secured on the wrong side and, although, it may seem unnecessary, do check that there are no missed stitches or beads. This is particularly important in a design incorporating many different colours or shades.

If possible, press the work on the wrong side, face downwards, over several clean towels or layers of folded blanket. Lay a clean tea towel or sheet over the wrong side of the work and press very lightly. Do not use steam unless absolutely necessary and make sure that the fabric behind the beads is absolutely dry before mounting behind glass. Do not use steam if silk has been included, as the tiny drops of water may mark the fabric.

If the work has distorted, measure and pin out on a cork board or carpet and leave for a few days to settle.

It is then necessary to decide how the finished work is to be displayed. The frame and mount should complement the piece itself. You may like to consult a professional framer. A very textured and beaded piece is probably better framed without glass. Information on care of textiles framed in this way can be found on pages 130–131.

A traditionally worked piece might look best in an antique frame and these can be picked up from antique fairs and jumble sales. It may be wise to treat any such purchase with woodworm treatment before use. Old wooden frames can be cleaned with a proprietary cleaner, or with fine wire wool soaked in white spirit. The frame should be left to dry thoroughly after treatment before being used.

A modern, experimental piece may be enhanced by the use of a frame treated with a decorative technique such as stencilling, ragging or sponging. While if using a mount board, this could include a painted extension of the design itself, or just a simple gold line.

Mounting the work without a frame

Materials

mount board	masking tape
cutting board	hammer
cotton sheeting (optional)	short tacks
craft knife fitted with a fresh blade	screw eyes
metal ruler	hanging cord
fabric adhesive	picture hooks

Method

1 Cut the mount board to the required size using the metal ruler and craft knife. The thickness of the mount board will depend on the size of the finished work and its weight. Thick modelling card should be suitable for most small pieces, while hardboard may be necessary for large designs. Obviously hardboard will need to be cut professionally to ensure that the edges are smooth and straight. Blockboard, plywood, chipboard and straw-board can also be used, but remember these will be heavier than the same thickness of hardboard.

2 If the fabric of the work is fine, cover the mount board with a layer of cotton sheeting, stretched and tacked into place.

3 Press the work and mark the centre point of all edges, using coloured tacking stitches or glass headed pins.

4 Measure and mark the centre of all sides of the mount board.

5 Lay a clean sheet over a flat surface and place the embroidery face down-wards over this.

6 Place the mount board over the work, matching the centre marks on both.

7 Working the shorter edges first, fold over the fabric to the wrong side of the mount board and glue first side in position.

8 Leave to dry completely before glueing the second short edge, pulling the fabric gently into position and removing any wrinkles.

9 When both short edges are secure, fold over the first long edge, making sure that the corner is neatly mitred. Glue this edge in place and leave to dry thoroughly.

10 Making sure that the work sits squarely on the board, turn over and glue the second long edge, pulling the fabric taut as before. Leave to dry completely.

Once the work has been mounted the back can be neatened in two ways.

either

1 Masking tape can be cut and laid over the raw edges of all sides and stuck in position.

or

1 Cut a piece of straight-grained fabric such as calico or linen to the size of the mount board, with a seam allowance of 2.5 cm (1 in) all round.

2 Press the turnings to the wrong side and place fabric over the back of the mounted work, with raw edges facing inwards.

3 Slipstitch the folded edge of the backing cloth to the edges of the work using a strong linen or cotton thread and tiny oversewing stitches.

Hanging the design

1 Attach two small curtain rings to the backing cloth parallel to the top edges of the work.

2 Thread a piece of cord between the two rings for hanging and knot securely.

Double mounting

A mounted work can be set into a second, larger mount board, which forms a border to the design work and can enhance the colours and fabrics used.

Method

1 Cut two boards – one to the size of the embroidered work and one larger.

2 Follow the method given for covering a mount board, covering the smaller board with the embroidered work and the larger one with either the same base fabric or a toning or contrasting material. The larger board could also be painted, stencilled, stippled, etc. in a variety of complementary colours.

3 Neaten the back of both boards, using the tape method.

4 Centralize the smaller board over the larger and lightly mark the position with a soft lead pencil.

5 The smaller board can then be glued or stitched in position.

6 If the work is to be stitched together, use a strong thread and very small oversewing or ladder stitches. A curved upholstery needle is most useful for working these stitches.

7 Small curtain rings should be stitched to the wrong side of the larger mount as before to carry the hanging cord.

To preserve the colour intensity of the work, it should not be placed in direct sunlight or above any source of heat.

10
Making beads

It is perfectly possible to make beads at home and indeed many needleworkers do prefer to make these for use in special projects. Without access to a kiln, however, techniques are fairly limited, but nevertheless, beadmaking can prove to be both a satisfying and rewarding experiment.

A small selection of simple methods and ideas are given here, but a trip to a museum or reference library should produce many other interesting techniques.

Clay beads

Clay beads can be made at home, reproducing those discovered in early Egyptian burial chambers and tombs. For this type of bead any craft clay which will dry without the need for firing will prove satisfactory.

Method

1 Take a small piece of modelling clay and roll it between the hands until the required shape is achieved.

2 Texture by rolling against a cheese or nutmeg grater or press with a file.

3 When satisfied with the results, pierce each bead with a needle or skewer and leave to dry naturally.

4 Once dry they can be painted or varnished (see page 126).

For a more professional effect, modern modelling mediums such as 'Fimo' can be used to produce beads in the same manner. These can be fired in a domestic oven. Experiment by rolling two or more colours together for a marbled effect, increasing the range of colour options available.

Salt dough beads

Salt dough modelling is extremely popular in America and Northern Europe. It evolved from the use of bread dough to make decorative items, such as harvest wheatsheafs. It is cheap and simple to produce and can be used, in much the same way as clay, to make unique and individual beads, which can be painted and varnished giving a wide range of finishes.

Ingredients

4 oz (100 g) plain white flour
2 oz (50 g) cooking salt
2 tsp (10 ml) wallpaper-paste
3 fl oz (75 ml) lukewarm water
1 tsp (5 ml) cooking oil

Method

1 Put measured flour, salt and wallpaper-paste into a large bowl and stir well.

2 Mix together the water and cooking oil in a small jug.

3 Pour water and oil onto dry ingredients, stirring well.

4 Turn the mixture out onto a work surface and knead for ten minutes, until thoroughly blended.

5 Place in a plastic bag and leave in a cool place for at least one hour.

6 Before shaping into beads, knead thoroughly until supple and crack free. If the mixture seems a little dry, knead in a few more drops of oil.

7 Shape beads by rolling between palms of the hands or on a flat surface.

8 Add any incised decoration using a skewer or bodkin.

9 Carefully pierce each bead with a darning needle, reshaping if necessary.

10 Place on a baking sheet and dry in a slow oven 50°C/130°F/Gas 1–2 overnight. Slow drying will help prevent cracking. As a further precaution, it may be advisable to prop open the oven door slightly.

11 Check beads are dry by tapping gently on a hard surface. They should sound hollow. If in doubt leave to dry for a while longer.

12 Once the beads are dry they can be painted or varnished.

Salt dough can be coloured before baking, with food colouring or powder paints, but colours will darken during the drying process.

Painting and varnishing clay or salt dough beads

Watercolour paints can be used either individually or in a variety of colours. For a cleaner, brighter effect, paint each bead with a white, acrylic based paint before the finishing colours are applied.

Enamel paints will give beads a high gloss finish, but these are more difficult to use and will take some time to dry. Beads to be painted with enamel paint should be held on cocktail sticks or skewers pushed into plasticine. The small pots of modeller's enamel are particularly suitable for this type of work and can be purchased in a wide range of colours.

Acrylic paints come in a variety of strong colours and are excellent for decorating beads. They are non-toxic and wash easily from brushes using cold running water. Acrylic paints also dry quickly and do not run.

Gold and silver paint for special effects can be brought from most good artist supply shops.

Beads can be left unpainted and unvarnished, or unpainted and varnished with a matt or gloss finish. Any painted beads should be left to dry very thoroughly before being varnished. Remember that two or three thin coats will give a far better finish than just one thick coat. Aerosol sprays seem to be an easy option, but in practice these will not produce a good finish and are difficult to use satisfactorily on small objects. Beads that have been painted and varnished will be more durable than those left in their natural dried state.

Rose petal beads

Perfumed beads were particularly popular during the seventeenth and eighteenth centuries, when gentlewomen would retire to the still-room to produce the herbal necessities of daily life. Many recipe books of the time give instructions for making beads from exotic ingredients such as civet, musk and ambergris. The unsatisfactory sanitary arrangements of the time, meant that the inclusion of perfume where possible was a necessary requirement and a string of perfumed beads would be a welcome accessory.

Scented beads have been made since Medieval times and the following recipe can be adapted for use with any heavily scented petals.

Method

1 Pick a large quantity of heavily scented rose petals. This is best done during the early morning on a dry summer day.

2 Put into the bowl of an electric blender and reduce to a pulp.

3 Spread the pulp onto a large flat earthenware or glass dish and leave in the refrigerator.

4 Repeat this process for the next few days.

5 Leave for a further 24 hours in a cool place without adding any more petals.

6 Mould the pulp into bead shapes between the palms of the hands.

7 Leave to dry again for 24 hours before piercing with a bodkin or darning needle.

8 Put onto a baking tray and dry in a slow oven (see instructions for salt dough beads).

Do remember that these beads will shrink quite noticeably when dried and make allowance for this when forming the hole. Pale coloured rose petals will brown as they dry, but dark red and crimson will keep their colour quite well.

Papier-mâché beads

Papier-mâché might, at first, seem a strange choice for bead making, but it is possible to experiment with a wide range of gift wrap and luxury papers to produce some interesting effects.

Method

1 Decide whether newspaper, gift wrap or tissue paper is to be used.

2 Tear this into tiny pieces and put into a plastic bucket or bowl.

3 Add just enough warm water to soak the paper.

4 Leave to stand for 30 minutes.

5 Squeeze out excess moisture.

6 Stir in a tablespoon of wallpaper-paste powder.

7 When stiff form into beads. If it is not stiff enough, continue to add a little wallpaper-paste powder until the correct consistency is achieved.

8 When all the beads are shaped, pierce with a needle or skewer and set on a lined baking sheet to dry.

9 Finished beads can be sanded smooth, before being painted or varnished (see facing page).

Paper beads

Paper beads are simple to make and can be used in embroidery projects which will not be required to withstand a great deal of wear and tear. Any type of paper can be used. Metallic giftwraps can look particularly attractive.

Method

1 Decide on the width of each bead and cut strips of paper accordingly.

2 Paste these one at a time with wallpaper-paste or craft glue, leaving a short length unpasted at one end.

3 Roll each strip round a knitting needle, starting with the unpasted end.

4 Leave to dry thoroughly before sliding from needle.

Beads can be painted and varnished or simply left as they are. They can also be rolled at an angle to produce different shapes and effects.

Wound wire beads

Fine copper wire can be wound round a fine knitting needle to make small beads. Or large wooden beads can be wound with wire which produces a customized decoration. When completed, the wire should be snipped close to the bead and the end turned in using fine-nosed pliers.

Tiny beads can be threaded onto copper wire to decorate a large bead as in the lacemaker's 'bird cage' spangle.

Silk wound beads

Large wooden beads can also be decorated with silk or metallic embroidery thread. The thread can be wound over the bead and through the hole, either in sections or covering the bead completely.

A fine crochet hook can be used to form a web of netting which can also be used to encase the bead. It can then be sewn in position, using the working thread.

Beads from everyday items

Beads for modern work can be made from many everyday items. Obviously pebbles and shells, which already have holes can be used, as can dried grass stalks, seed heads and large seeds. Any of these can be gilded, painted or varnished. Seed heads and grass stalks should be pierced before being dried to prevent cracking. Dried seeds can be soaked in fresh cooking oil before being pierced. Those that prove difficult to pierce can be drilled with a fine ratchet drill or pierced with a red hot needle, although both operations require extreme care.

Any form of fine tubing can be cut into lengths and strung as beads.

Pasta shapes

The many varieties of pasta shapes can be used as beading in certain pieces. Experiment with paints and varnishes to achieve the required results. Oil based paints are most suitable for this, although drying times will be long.

Vegetable peelings

A seemingly unlikely choice might be fine peelings of root vegetables, such as carrot, swede and parsnip. These can be left to dry, either in the airing cupboard or in a slow oven. They will contort into strange shapes which can be combined with experimental work. Peelings are best couched into position, although before drying a number can be threaded onto a skewer.

11
Care of beadwork

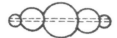

A considerable amount of work goes into the production of beaded work and, therefore, it deserves special treatment to preserve its beauty for as long as possible.

Antique beaded textiles can present a problem and so, in this chapter, advice is given on gentle care and conservation which can be undertaken at home.

In the case of jewellery and beaded garments, these should always be put on after using damaging substances such as perfume or hairspray. Even foundation cream and, of course, lipstick, can present a problem, so it is advisable to cover the face with a chiffon scarf when putting on a special dress or blouse.

Never swim in jewellery. Chlorine, salt and even water can severely damage beads, whilst weakening the stringing threads.

Cleaning beads

In order to clean beads effectively, it is necessary to be sure of the material involved. It is then a simple matter of choosing the most appropriate method. The golden rule is, however, if in any doubt, do not attempt home cleaning, take the beads to a reputable jeweller for his advice.

The surface of many decorative beads may be destroyed by the use of white spirit or other solvents. This is particularly true of many antique finishes. It is worth remembering that the appeal of many of these is enhanced by the patina acquired over the years and this should not be destroyed.

Pottery and glass

Glazed pottery, porcelain and glass beads can be gently washed in lukewarm, soapy water. They should then be placed on a clean towel and left to dry naturally. Antique beads should be wiped over very carefully with a dampened cloth, as water may perish the stringing threads.

Wooden beads

Well-polished wooden beads can be cleaned with a dampened, soapy cloth, dried thoroughly and lightly polished with beeswax. Very dirty old beads can be treated with one of the proprietory wood cleaners and restorers that are now available from hardware shops.

Unpolished coarse-grained wooden beads should be wiped over with a bare damp cloth, as any excess water will be absorbed and may swell the grain.

Pearls, amber and jet

Apart from being wiped occasionally with a soft cloth, the cleaning of pearls, amber and jet is best left to an expert. All these natural materials should be worn frequently, as the natural oils of the skin help to keep them in good condition.

The storing of beads

Valuable beads and beaded fabrics should be stored correctly to preserve them, wherever possible, from atmospheric changes, light and pollution.

Beaded jewellery

Each item should be stored separately in individual soft fabric pouches where possible.

Semi-precious stones

Semi-precious stones such as aquamarine, opal, amethyst and turquoise should be wrapped in acid-free tissue and stored away from light and heat, which will, in time, fade their colour.

Pearls, amber and jet

As has already been said, these natural substances should be worn often. Drying and lack of light and air will cause their surfaces to crack and ultimately disintegrate. As with other beads, they will be damaged by cosmetics, hairspray and perfume and should, therefore, be protected from these substances.

All good quality necklaces and bracelets should be restrung frequently using silk thread.

Beaded textiles

The storing of beaded textiles, and garments in particular, can present a variety of problems.

Small items can be stored flat, wrapped in acid-free tissue paper in boxes or light-free drawers. If using wooden drawers, these should first be lined with acid-free tissue paper, which will help prevent fabric fibres disintegrating and reduce fading. These should be kept flat away from the light. Do not store any fabrics in plastic or polythene bags or containers. Plastic and polythene will hold humidity which will provide ideal conditions for the growth of mould and mildew. In addition, polythene attracts dust which can dirty items being stored. Cellophane can be used, but it has the disadvantage of tearing easily.

Fabric covers such as pillow cases and specially made dust sheets are suitable for larger items.

Dresses to be stored flat should be stuffed with acid-free tissue paper, to avoid unnecessary creases and folds, which will subject the ground threads to additional stress.

Dresses, jackets and blouses can be stored on hangers, which have been well padded with cotton wool and covered with calico or cotton. The garment can then be further protected with a dust sheet of calico or cotton. Never hang a beaded garment from an unpadded hanger. Stuff the sleeves, bodice and upper part of the skirt with crumpled tissue paper and, if necessary, stitch tapes to the inside of the skirt to the top of the hanger to help ease the weight on the fabric of the bodice.

It is important, when storing more than one item that they be well spaced, to minimize creasing. Tie a label to the top of each bag to identify the garment it contains.

A very heavily beaded garment or one with its fabric cut on the cross should always be stored flat, or it will drop out of shape. Line a cardboard box with acid-free tissue paper and layer more above and below the garment. Tissue paper should also be crumpled into bodice and sleeves.

Any particularly sharp or large beads should be surrounded by tissue paper or cotton wool to protect the fabric on which it sits.

Examine all beaded work regularly and check for signs of attack by moths.

Cleaning beadwork

Fragile antique or modern beadwork should be cleaned professionally.

On household textiles, vacuum cleaning is possible to remove accumulations of dust. Cover the upholstery nozzle of the cleaner with a piece of nylon monofilament screening and gently move over the surface of the fabric. The screening will prevent the fibres of the textile being picked up, but will draw through dust particles.

Brushing of beaded textiles is not recommended, as too vigorous an application can dislodge beads and threads. However, the old-fashioned method of cleaning with a goose feather or sable paint brush can be employed before vacuuming with a nylon screen.

Washing old, beaded textiles is a method which can only be considered for items which are of no intrinsic or historical value and should only be used as a last resort.

Appendix

Bead shapes

Plain

These are usually round or tubular with a smooth surface.

Rocaille

Rocaille beads are round inside and out. They can be opaque, transparent, metallic, opaline (smooth and glossy), iridescent, lustred, pearlized, silverlined, frosted, iris.

Tabular

Tabular beads are flat, the hole is drilled through each bead. They can be round, square or hexagonal.

Annular

These are ring-shaped beads.

Oblate

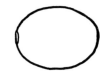

These measure more round the diameter than the length.

Bugle

Bugle beads are tiny glass tubes which can vary in length from 2–35 mm. The outside of the bugle can be smooth or ridged. These beads can be transparent or opaque and, for added sparkle, can be lined with gold or silver.

Cylindrical

These include faceted, square, barrel and both curved tubes and straight tubes.

Tosca

Tosca beads are smooth outside, but square cut inside to catch the light. They are also known as 'square rocailles'.

Charlotte

Charlotte or three cut beads are faceted in three ways on the outside. These beads can also be cut on the inside and lined with metal foil.

Two cut

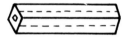

Two cut beads are cut inside and out and are square (almost like small bugle beads).

Faceted

These beads have many cut sides and come in a variety of shapes including round, oval and teardrop.

Rosettes

These flower-shaped cut glass or plastic beads come in a variety of colours and sizes.

Marguerites

Another form of flower bead, marguerites have distinctive indentations marking their petals.

Drops and pendants

These are pear and heart-shaped and are made from cut-glass.

Cones

There are a great many variations of cone-shaped beads including; long convex cones, convex cone discs, bicones (having a cone shape at either end), round bicones, short convex bicones, truncated bicones, fluted bicones and truncated bicones.

Cornerless cubes

Available in a variety of colours, in glass, wood or plastic, cornerless cubes are useful in jewellery and for experimental work.

Unusual shapes

There are a great many other shapes which beads are made into including; melon-shaped, lentil-shaped, fluted, cog, rayed, discs, ellipsoid. The diagram includes pyramid, triangle, hexagon, lozenge and diamond shape.

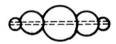

Segmented

Glass, plastic or metallic beads are available in various shapes and colours and are distinguished by their waisted appearance.

Indian glass

Indian glass beads are available up to 50 mm in length and are transparent with coloured stripes or twisted and striped like old-fashioned barley sugar sticks.

Lamp

Glass lamp beads are still made by traditional methods in India. They are recognised by their colours and distinctive designs.

Miscellaneous bead shapes

Some of these beads include wire hoops from which the bead can be hung. Shapes are varied and include; leaves, bananas, miniature dolls, dolphins, strawberries and oranges.

Societies

United States

Without any national organization, there are numerous independent BEAD SOCIETIES covering virtually every region. A list of these as well as other resources can be found in the following directories.

THOSE BAD BAD BEADS, Virginia Blakelock
Available from Universal Synergetics and Lacis as listed opposite

THE BEAD DIRECTORY
Write: PO Box 10103, Oakland, CA 94610

CENTRE FOR THE STUDY OF BEADWORK
3734 NE 35th Ave.
PO Box 13719
Portland, OR 97213-0719

United Kingdom

BEAD SOCIETY OF GREAT BRITAIN
Open to any individual or professional interested in any aspect of bead work from any perspective. Formed in 1989, the society holds five meetings each year offering lectures, workshops and bazaars as well as publishing five newsletters.

Carole Morris, Secretary
THE BEAD SOCIETY OF GREAT BRITAIN
1 Casburn Lane
Burwell,
Cambridgeshire CB5 0ED

Suppliers

United States

Universal Synergetics
16510 SW Edminston Rd.
Wilsonville, OR 97070-9514

Lacis
2982 Adeline Street
Berkeley, CA 94703
Tambour supplies, books, threads and ribbons

Ornamental Resources
1427 Miner Street
Idaho Springs, CO 80452

Shipwreck Beads
5021 Mud Bay Road
Olympia, WA 98502
Wholesale and retail

Magnum's
PO Box 362
Blackfoot, ID 83221
Specializing in old beads

General Bead
1010 Broadway
San Diego, CA 92101

Beadazzled
1522 Connecticut Ave. NW
Washington DC 20036

Garden of Beadin'
PO Box 1535
Redway, CA 95542

United Kingdom

The Bead Shop,
43 Neal Street,
London WC2H 9PJ

Creative Beadcraft Ltd.
Unit 26,
Chiltern Trading Estate,
Earl Hower Road
Holmer Green
High Wycombe
Buckinghamshire HP15 5QT

Ells and Farrier Ltd,
20 Princes Street,
Hanover Square,
London W1R 7RG

Creative Beadcraft Ltd,
Denmark Works,
Sheepcote Dell Road,
Beamond End,
Near Amersham,
Buckinghamshire HP7 ORX

Spangles
1 Casburn Lane
Burwell
Cambridgeshire CB5 0ED

Places to visit

United States

Brooklyn Museum
200 Eastern Parkway
Brooklyn, NY 11238

Costume Institute
Metropolitan Museum of Art, the
Fifth Avenue and 82nd Street
New York, NY 10028

Smithsonian Institution,
Washington DC 20560

Museum of the City of New York
Fifth Avenue at 103rd Street
New York, NY 10029

Canada

Royal Ontario Museum,
100 Queen's Park,
Toronto
Ontario M5S 2C6

United Kingdom

British Museum
Great Russell Street
London WC1B 3DG

Victoria and Albert Museum,
Cromwell Road
South Kensington,
London SW7 2RL

Embroiderers' Guild Collection,
Apartment 41,
Hampton Court Palace,
Surrey KT8 9AU
081 977 8441 (telephone appointments
necessary)

Museum of Costume and Textiles
51 Castle Gate
Nottingham NG1 6AP

Further Reading

Alibeck, Tahia *Be-dazzling!*, Alibeck, 1992

Bowman, Sara *A Fashion for Extravagance*, Bell & Hyman, London, 1985

Budwig, Robert, and Coles, Janet *The Complete Book of Beads*, Dorling Kindersley, London, 1990

Campbell–Harding, Valerie and Watts, Pamela *Bead Embroidery*, Lacis, 1993

Classification and Nomenclature of Beads and Pendants George Shumway, Pennsylvania, 1973

Coles, Janet & Dudwig, Robert *The Book of Beads*, Simon & Schuster, 1990

Edwards, Joan *Bead Embroidery*, Lacis, 1992

Erikson, Joan Mowat *The Universal Bead* W. W. Norton & Co. Inc., New York, 1969

Finch, Karen, and Putman, Greta *Caring and Preservation of Textiles*, Lacis, 1991

Goodhue, Horace *Indian Bead-Weaving Patterns*, Beadcraft, 1971

Hériteau, Jacqueline *Potpourris and Other Fragrant Delights*, Penguin, London, 1978

Huetson, T. L. *Lace and Bobbins*, David and Charles, Newton Abbot, 1973

Jarratt, Maisie *Embroidery Beading Designs and Techniques*, Kangaroo, 1992

Jarratt, Maisie *How to Bead; French Embroidery Beading*, Kangaroo, 1990

Kliot, Jules & Kaethe *Bead Work*, Lacis, 1984

Mackrell, Alice *Paul Poiret*, Batsford, 1990

de Marley, Diana *The History of Haute Couture*, Batsford, London, 1980

Moss, Kathlyn & Scherer, Alice *The New Beadwork*, Abrams, 1992

Sako, Takako, *Classic Bead Weaving* (Japanese text), NHK, Tokyo 1988

Springett, Christine and David *Spangles and Superstitions*, published by authors, 1987

Swift, Gay *The Batsford Book of Embroidery Techniques* Batsford, 1984

Thompson, Angela *Embroidery with Beads*, Lacis, 1987

Van der Steen, W. G. N. *A Handbook on Beads* George Shumway, Pennsylvania

White, Mary *How to do Beadwork*, (Doubleday, 1904) Dover, 1972

LACIS publishes and distributes books specifically related to the textile arts, focusing on the subjects of lace and lace making, costume, embroidery, needlepoint and hand sewing.

LACIS books of interest:

BEAD EMBROIDERY, Joan Edwards
BEAD EMBROIDERY, Valerie Campbell-Harding and Pamela Watts
EMBROIDERY WITH BEADS, Angela Thompson
BEADWORK, Jules & Kaethe Kliot
THE ART OF TATTING, Katherine Hoare
TATTING WITH VISUAL PATTERNS, Mary Konior
THE ART OF SHETLAND LACE, Sarah Don
THE ART OF HAIR WORK; HAIR BRAIDING AND JEWELRY OF
    SENTIMENT, Mark Campbell
THE CARE AND PRESERVATION OF TEXTILES, Karen Finch & Greta
    Putnam
THE ART OF DRAWN WORK, Metropolian Art
THE ART OF NETTING, Jules & Kaethe Kliot
FASHION OUTLINES, Margaret C. Ralston
LADIES' TAILOR-MADE GARMENTS 1908, S. S. Gordon
"STANDARD" WORK ON CUTTING (MEN'S GARMENTS): 1886
MILLINERY FOR EVERY WOMAN, Georgina Kerr Kaye
THE BARGELLO BOOK Frances Salter

For a complete list of LACIS titles, write to:

LACIS
3163 Adeline Street
Berkeley, CA 94703
USA

Index